I.S. 61 Library

I.S. 61 Library

I.S. 61 Librar

YOU
ARE THE
JUROR

GREAT DECISIONS

You
Are the
Juror

Nathan Aaseng

The Oliver Press, Inc.
Minneapolis

The Oliver Press, Inc.
Charlotte Square
5707 West 36th Street
Minneapolis, MN 55416-2510

Library of Congress Cataloging-in-Publication Data

Aaseng, Nathan.
You are the juror / Nathan Aaseng.
p.   cm.—(Great decisions)
Includes bibliographical references and index.
    Summary: The reader assumes the role of a juror in eight
famous trials of the twentieth century: the Lindbergh kidnapping,
Sullivan v. New York Times, the Chicago Seven, Patty Hearst's
trial for armed robbery, and others.
ISBN 1-881508-40-4 (lib. bdg.)
1. Trials—United States—Juvenile literature.   2. Jury—United
States—Juvenile literature.   [1. Trials. 2. Jury. 3. Decision
making.]   I. Title. II. Series: Great decisions (Minneapolis,
Minn.)
KF220.A18   1997
345.73'07—DC21   96-53046
                                                         CIP
                                                          AC

Great Decisions VIII
Printed in the United States of America

08 07 06 05 04 03 02   8 7 6 5 4 3 2

CONTENTS

Although the American jury system was adopted from British law, juries are much more powerful in the United States than in Great Britain, largely due to a rebellious tradition that began with the case pictured above. In a process called jury nullification, *the jurors in the 1735 John Peter Zenger trial defied the law and acquitted a printer for publishing anti-British stories in his newspaper. Juries still hold the right to acquit defendants charged under a law jurors feel is unjust.*

INTRODUCTION

The fate of a human being is in your hands. Standing, the defendant nervously awaits your judgment. You are a juror, and one word from you and the 11 other members of the jury can cause the accused to win freedom or to suffer punishments that include fines, jail sentences, or even death.

In the course of the trial, several key players command your attention. The judge runs the proceedings and keeps order in the court. The prosecutor presents evidence that the defendant is guilty of the crime. The defense attorney presents evidence that the accused is not guilty. Witnesses testify as to what they have seen, heard, or concluded about the case. As a juror, you must sift through the conflicting testimony and evidence that both the prosecution and the defense present to you. You must decide if witnesses are telling the truth, if experts know what they are talking about, and if the conclusions that the attorneys draw make sense.

Unfortunately, you do not have the freedom of a reporter or a historian to uncover the facts of the case. In the legal system in the United States, the only evidence you may consider is that which the attorneys bring before

You might have a hard time keeping track of all the lawyers and witnesses in courtrooms of high-profile cases like the Lindbergh kidnapping trial. Defense attorney Edward J. Reilly (in glasses) chats with prosecutor David T. Wilentz (shuffling papers) while defendant Bruno Hauptmann (at right) looks on warily.

you. A prosecutor may fail to ask a crucial question. A defense attorney may neglect to produce an important piece of evidence. For any number of legal technicalities, a judge may bar certain testimony that would help you to reach a conclusion. Your decision must be made solely on the basis of the evidence the attorneys for the prosecution and the defense present at the trial.

Jury duty can be a thankless task. Many people read about famous trials and form their own opinions about the defendant's guilt or innocence. Your decision may infuriate those who do not agree with you. Nevertheless, these other people are not the jurors. That job is yours. Our system of justice demands that you ignore popular opinion and base your decision only on the evidence. But even when you do that, lawyers may appeal to a higher court, which may overrule the verdict that you reach.

The pressure of jury duty can be unbearable. After the trial, you may wonder if you sentenced an innocent person to jail or even to death. But you must remember that the accused has many opportunities to appeal to a higher court and overturn a guilty verdict. If you find someone not guilty who is truly guilty, however, our legal system offers no remedy. The criminal will go free because the law prohibits trying a person twice in criminal courts for the same crime.

The jury in the 1925 "Scopes Monkey Trial" was under the scrutiny of spectators crowded in the hot courtroom. These observers already had decided whether John Scopes should be punished for teaching the theory of evolution.

The United States puts a greater percentage of people behind bars each year than any other industrialized nation. The prisoner population in federal prisons, such as Leavenworth Penitentiary, is growing at a much faster rate than in state prisons, largely because of mandatory, or required, sentences in federal drug-related crimes.

Within the pages of this book, you will reach judgments on some of the most famous and controversial cases ever to come before a jury. The crimes range from kidnapping and murder to robbery, libel, and conspiracy to incite a riot.

Seven of the cases you will judge involve criminal complaints—those in which the defendant is accused of committing a crime. In a criminal case, the prosecution carries the burden of proof. Prosecutors must convince you beyond a reasonable doubt that the accused is guilty of the charges. If you think the evidence shows only that the defendant might have committed the crime, you must vote not guilty. The eighth case involves a civil suit, in which one person sues another person for causing a personal injury. Here the standard of proof is somewhat more lenient. Two of the criminal cases in this book, the

Bernhard Goetz trial for attempted murder and the O. J. Simpson trial for murder, have also been tried separately as civil cases when the families of the victims filed suits against these defendants.

This book can give you only a partial experience of what a juror goes through. Most of these trials lasted for weeks, some for months. In several of the cases, the juries were *sequestered*, or kept isolated, from the media and the public in hotel rooms for the duration of the trial. Written records of the testimony go on for hundreds,

The sequestered jurors in the Ford Pinto trial for reckless homicide spent some of their time outside the courtroom putting jigsaw puzzles together.

even thousands, of pages. You will not have the opportunity to read all this testimony in the following pages. And, unlike the real jurors in these cases, you will not be able to hear the voices of the witnesses or study their faces for clues as to whether they are honest and reliable.

What this book will present are the most important arguments and evidence in the eight cases. As in a real trial, the prosecutors will make their case first. Then the defense attorneys will argue their case. In some trials, prosecutors will *rebut*, or challenge the accuracy of, crucial arguments that the defense makes. Finally, the judge will offer brief instruction as to how the law applies to the case in question. After that, the verdict is up to you.

As a last chance for their clients, lawyers in the United States who are unhappy with the rulings in lower courts may try to appeal, *or bring their cases, to the U.S. Supreme Court—the highest court in the land.*

1

BRUNO HAUPTMANN
THE LINDBERGH KIDNAPPING
1935

In 1927, as the first person to make a solo airplane flight across the Atlantic Ocean from New York to Paris, Charles Lindbergh became perhaps the most popular hero in the world and was hailed by crowds everywhere. But nearly five years after his legendary flight, glory turned to tragedy.

On the night of March 1, 1932, Charles and Anne Morrow Lindbergh's 20-month-old son, Charles Augustus Lindbergh III, disappeared from their country mansion near Hopewell, New Jersey. In a note marred by poor spelling and grammar, the kidnapper demanded $50,000 in small bills. "We warn you," the note threatened, "for making anyding public or for the polise."

Eventually, the Lindberghs received a total of 15 written messages with instructions as to how to proceed with paying the ransom. Charles Lindbergh delivered

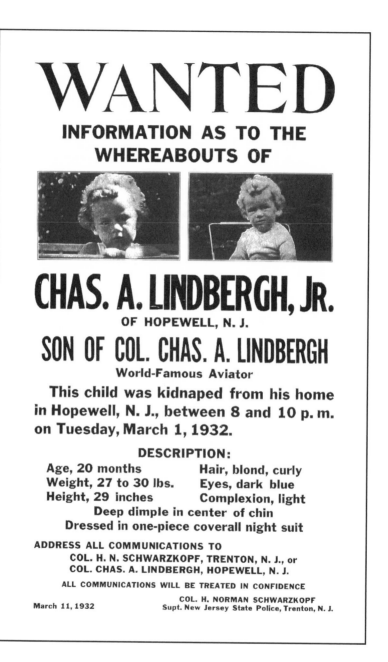

WANTED

INFORMATION AS TO THE WHEREABOUTS OF

CHAS. A. LINDBERGH, JR.

OF HOPEWELL, N. J.

SON OF COL. CHAS. A. LINDBERGH

World-Famous Aviator

This child was kidnaped from his home in Hopewell, N. J., between 8 and 10 p. m. on Tuesday, March 1, 1932.

DESCRIPTION:

Age, 20 months   Hair, blond, curly
Weight, 27 to 30 lbs.   Eyes, dark blue
Height, 29 inches   Complexion, light
Deep dimple in center of chin
Dressed in one-piece coverall night suit

ADDRESS ALL COMMUNICATIONS TO
COL. H. N. SCHWARZKOPF, TRENTON, N. J., or
COL. CHAS. A. LINDBERGH, HOPEWELL, N. J.

ALL COMMUNICATIONS WILL BE TREATED IN CONFIDENCE

March 11, 1932

COL. H. NORMAN SCHWARZKOPF
Supt. New Jersey State Police, Trenton, N. J.

When the baby of one of America's most famous celebrities vanished, it was national news. Although calls offering aid came from around the country, no one, it seemed, could help the Lindberghs find their son.

the money according to the kidnapper's instructions, but little Charles was not returned to his parents. On May 12, in the New Jersey woods only a little over two miles from the Lindberghs' home, a trucker found the body of a baby who had died from a blow to the head. Charles and Anne Morrow Lindbergh identified the child as their young son.

The first money displaying the serial number of one of the ransom bills turned up within a few days of the payment. But efforts by the police to trace the kidnapper through these serial numbers reached a dead end. Finally, more than two years after the crime, a gas-station attendant wrote down the car-license number of a man who paid for his gasoline with a $10 bill. The bill was one of those Lindbergh had given to the kidnapper.

Police investigators traced the license number to a 34-year-old German immigrant carpenter named Bruno Richard Hauptmann. Charged with murder by the state of New Jersey, Bruno Hauptmann went to trial on January 2, 1935.

THE CASE FOR THE PROSECUTION

In the trial, David T. Wilentz, the New Jersey state attorney general, laid out the incriminating evidence against Hauptmann. A key witness for the prosecution was Dr. John Condon, a retired teacher and principal from New York City who had served as a contact between Charles Lindbergh and the kidnapper.

Acting on instructions from the caller, Condon met a man who identified himself only as "John." To prove that he had the baby, the man agreed to hand over the child's sleeper, and he mailed it to Condon several days later. At another meeting, "John" accepted the ransom payment in exchange for directions to where authorities could find the baby. (The directions proved to be false.)

In the trial, Dr. Condon identified Hauptmann as "Cemetery John" by his voice. Like "John," Hauptmann had a strong German accent. Charles Lindbergh had accompanied Condon on this second meeting with "John." Lindbergh testified that while waiting in the car on a dark evening outside St. Raymond's Cemetery in New York City, he heard the man shout, "Hey, Doctor! Over here!" The voice sounded identical to that of Bruno Richard Hauptmann, Lindbergh claimed.

Charles Lindbergh answers questions on the witness stand during the trial of Bruno Hauptmann, the suspected kidnapper and murderer of his son.

The gas-station attendant testified that Hauptmann had paid for his gasoline with one of the ransom bills. In addition, police investigators testified that they found in the garage behind Hauptmann's apartment nearly $14,000 worth of bills wrapped in an old newspaper. Serial numbers identified the bills as those given to the Lindbergh kidnapper. Yet Hauptmann had told them he had no other ransom money in his possession.

During the course of the investigation before the trial, the police had uncovered many details linking Hauptmann to the crime as well as incidents that made him look suspicious. When they asked him if he had a criminal record, Hauptmann lied that he did not. In fact, he had served three years in a German prison for felonies such as armed robbery.

The prosecution introduced work records showing Hauptmann had quit his job as a carpenter at about the time the Lindberghs had paid the ransom. An accountant testified that Hauptmann deposited considerable sums of money in his bank account shortly after leaving his job. Attorney General Wilentz asked the jurors to consider the odds that these events were merely coincidental.

Several handwriting experts swore under oath that the same person had written all the ransom notes and that the handwriting style matched Hauptmann's. Also, in one memo Hauptmann had written for police, he had written "boad" for the word "boat"—just as the kidnapper had done in one of the ransom notes.

A taxi driver took the stand for the prosecution to testify that Hauptmann had paid him a dollar to deliver a message to Condon. Three separate witnesses placed Hauptmann in the vicinity of the Lindbergh house around the date of the crime. One of them said he saw a ladder in the back of the car that Hauptmann was driving.

After the kidnapping, police had found such a ladder lying about 70 feet away from the house. During his testimony, woodworking expert Arthur Koehler stated that he had traced the lumber used to make the ladder to a store in the Bronx, New York. Police found evidence that Hauptmann had used a board from his own attic to build one of the rails of the ladder. Furthermore, investigators found Dr. Condon's phone number scrawled on the wall of a closet in Hauptmann's house.

Facing the jury, prosecutor Wilentz argued that he had presented overwhelming evidence to prove that Hauptmann, acting alone, had kidnapped and murdered 20-month-old Charles Augustus Lindbergh III.

The ladder police believe was used by the kidnapper leans against the Lindberghs' mansion as investigators examine other evidence at the crime scene.

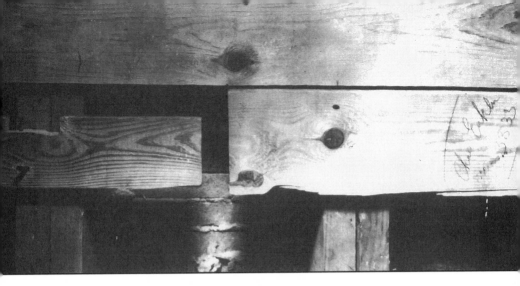

The gap in the floor of Bruno Hauptmann's attic.
Police matched a rail in the ladder found at the crime
scene to the missing floorboard.

THE CASE FOR THE DEFENSE

Attorney Edward J. Reilly prepared the defense. Bruno Hauptmann and his wife provided an alibi for the evening of the kidnapping. Hauptmann had picked up his wife when she finished her shift at a bakery, and the two were together the rest of the night. Three witnesses supported their claim, saying they had seen Hauptmann at the bakery on the evening of the kidnapping.

Other witnesses stated that on April 2, 1932, the day that Condon had given the ransom money to "Cemetery John," Hauptmann had gone home after work to entertain a friend, who came over at seven o'clock. Reilly observed that Hauptmann would not have had time to go to the cemetery to meet with Condon.

On the witness stand, Hauptmann explained why he happened to have so much of the kidnapper's money. He had been involved in a fur and stock-trading business with a man named Isador Fisch. In December 1933,

While he was in custody during the kidnapping trial, Bruno Hauptmann had to be away from his wife and his own young son.

Fisch had asked Hauptmann to hold some of his belongings while Fisch traveled to Germany to visit his parents. One of the items was a shoebox.

Several witnesses reported seeing Fisch give Hauptmann the shoebox for safekeeping, but none of them had seen what was in the box. Hauptmann himself maintained he had no idea the box contained money until Fisch died while still in Europe. After he opened the box, Hauptmann decided to keep the money to pay off a large debt that Fisch had owed him. In August 1934, he began to spend the money.

Hauptmann denied having any knowledge of Condon's telephone number. When asked about the ladder he allegedly had built, Hauptmann stated indignantly, "I am a carpenter," indicating he would not have built such a crude ladder. Defense attorney Reilly cast doubt as to whether the ladder on exhibit in the courtroom had actually been used in the kidnapping because it wasn't long enough. When leaned against the Lindberghs' house, it fell short of the nursery window.

The defense posed other questions casting doubt on the prosecution's story. Why would Hauptmann remove a piece of wood from his attic to build a ladder when he had a garage full of wood to use? Why hadn't the Lindberghs' dog barked the moment it sensed an intruder? Did not this absence of barking suggest that someone in the Lindbergh house, who would not have alarmed the dog, had played a role in the kidnapping?

The defense then produced financial records showing that Hauptmann's testimony about his finances was truthful. The large deposits to his bank account were the result of his stock-market dealings. When he made a profit by selling stocks, Hauptmann frequently would transfer money from one account to another.

The defense also pointed out that when Dr. Condon first saw Hauptmann at the police station, he did not identify him as "Cemetery John." Condon made the declaration only after the police began building a case against Hauptmann. And how could Lindbergh identify Hauptmann's voice as "Cemetery John's" after hearing the kidnapper utter only a few words two years ago?

Finally, the defense displayed evidence of a bank transaction involving nearly $3,000 of the marked ransom money. All of the handwriting experts agreed that the writing on the transaction slip was not Bruno Hauptmann's. This indicated that someone else had committed the crime.

THE PROSECUTION'S REBUTTAL

To refute defense testimony, the prosecution introduced a theater employee who said that on November 26, 1933, Hauptmann had paid for a movie ticket with one of the ransom bills. This had occurred well before Hauptmann claimed to have discovered Fisch's money.

One of the ransom bills found in Hauptmann's possession. Before the Lindberghs paid the $50,000 ransom, police recorded the serial numbers of the bills so the money could later be traced.

LEGAL ISSUES

According to New Jersey law, if the jurors found Hauptmann guilty, they had the option of recommending a sentence of life imprisonment. If they did not recommend this more lenient sentence, Judge Thomas Trenchard could impose the death penalty.

YOU ARE THE JUROR.
WHAT IS YOUR DECISION?

Gathered outside the building in which you are deliberating, a large, angry crowd chants "Baby-killer! Burn Hauptmann!" But you must make your own decision. What is your verdict in the murder and kidnapping charges against Bruno Richard Hauptmann?

Option 1 **Hauptmann is guilty, and the state should impose the death penalty.**

Option 2 **Hauptmann is guilty, and the state should impose life imprisonment.**

Option 3 **Hauptmann is not guilty.**

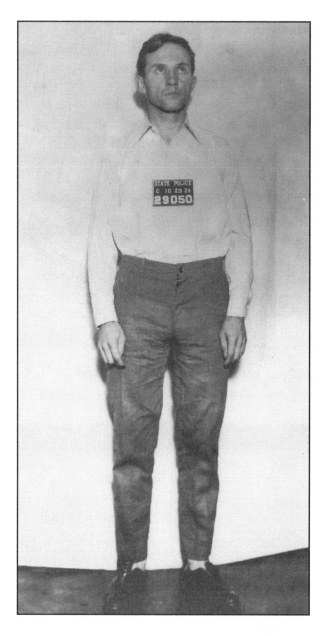

Bruno Hauptmann never wavered from his claim that he was innocent of the kidnapping and murder of young Charles Augustus Lindbergh III.

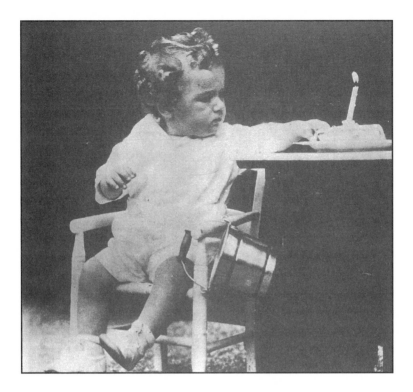

Charles A. Lindbergh III on his first birthday, eight months before his death at the hands of a kidnapper

The jurors chose *Option 1*. They found Hauptmann guilty and recommended death.

Almost immediately after entering the jury room, the eight men and four women on the jury voted for a guilty verdict. But they continued to deliberate for 11 hours about whether to recommend the death sentence. Eventually, two holdouts on the jury joined the majority, and Judge Thomas Trenchard sentenced Hauptmann to die in the electric chair. On April 3, 1936—one year, three months, and one day after his trial had begun—the state of New Jersey executed Bruno Richard Hauptmann.

Police had to hold back the crowds when Charles Lindbergh entered the courthouse in Flemington, New Jersey, during each day of the trial.

ANALYSIS

A large majority of Americans agreed with the verdict in the trial of Bruno Hauptmann. Yet the mob of people gathered in front of the courthouse disturbed many of those who supported the guilty verdict. No matter how passionate people feel about a case, attempts to intimidate a jury hurt the cause of justice. Even Charles Lindbergh expressed dismay at what he called "a lynching crowd."

A minority of Americans believed Hauptmann to be innocent, including New Jersey governor Harold Hoffman. His postponement of the death sentence—originally scheduled for March 18, 1935—and his attempt to further investigate the case angered many voters and cost him his political career.

Many others also harbored doubts about the case. Famed trial lawyer Clarence Darrow declared, "No man should be executed on such flimsy evidence." An *Editor and Publisher* article stated that "no trial in this century has so degraded the administration of justice," referring not only to the chanting mob, but also to the way in which both the state and the defense had presented their cases. Many experts agreed that Hauptmann's lawyer had given a rather halfhearted defense.

In the years after the trial's end, the following facts came to light:

1. A witness who told police that he had seen Hauptmann near the Lindbergh home was legally blind.

2. Another prosecution witness admitted to lying under oath for money.

3. Handwriting experts had based their demonstration of a "match" with the ransom letters on only a few sentences of the many samples of Hauptmann's writing available to them. Other handwriting experts, who were convinced that Hauptmann had not written the ransom notes, did not have the opportunity to appear in court.

4. Dr. Condon's telephone number had been written on the wall in Hauptmann's closet by a reporter, who then had prepared a story on the "new" evidence.

5. Private investigators traced the kidnapping to a man named Paul Wendel, who confessed (but later denied) that he was "Cemetery John."

6. Letters that police investigators had seized from Hauptmann confirmed his business relationship with Isador Fisch.

These and other issues have cast a cloud of controversy over the Lindbergh kidnapping case that lingers to this day. In recent years, Hauptmann has gained more sympathy. In 1994, author Noel Behn presented a compelling case that the supposed kidnapping never took place at all and that the baby had died two days earlier, probably at the hands of Charles Lindbergh's sister-in-law. The resulting report of a kidnapping, he argues, was merely a cover-up.

As with many court cases, the members of the jury in the Hauptmann trial had to live with their decision to condemn Bruno Richard Hauptmann to death, never knowing whether they had interpreted all the evidence correctly, or whether they had even seen and heard all the evidence that would have helped them to decide the case.

2

THE *NEW YORK TIMES*
A QUESTION OF LIBEL
1960

I n early 1960, the state of Alabama brought charges
against Dr. Martin Luther King Jr., accusing him of
filing fraudulent returns on his 1956 and 1958 income
taxes. Since the state had never before charged anyone
with felony income-tax evasion, King's supporters
believed Alabama officials were persecuting the black
leader for actively promoting civil rights.

A group of 64 prominent Americans, including former first lady Eleanor Roosevelt and actor Sidney Poitier,
formed the Committee to Defend Martin Luther King.
They quickly put together and paid for a full-page advertisement to raise money for King's defense.

The *New York Times* ran the advertisement, headed
"Heed Their Rising Voices," on March 29, 1960. The ad
described a number of incidents in which government
officials in southern states had attempted to silence

As Martin Luther King Jr. (second from right) rose to national prominence, he became a threat to racist white southerners. Here he meets in December 1955 with other activists to organize the Montgomery bus boycott to protest segregated seating on city buses.

supporters of equal rights for African Americans. One such incident concerned the expulsion of several students by Alabama State College in Montgomery, Alabama. The advertisement ended with a plea for money.

Even though he was not mentioned in the ad and was not responsible for the events the ad criticized, the *New York Times* advertisement offended L. B. Sullivan, one of the three elected commissioners of the city of Montgomery. He said it was libelous because it contained false statements that injured his reputation as an honest, capable government official. Sullivan filed a $500,000 suit against the *New York Times* for publishing the ad and against four black Alabama church leaders— Ralph D. Abernathy, S. S. Seay Sr., Fred Shuttlesworth, and J. E. Lowery—whose names appeared in the ad.

The case came to trial on November 1, 1960, in Montgomery. (Meanwhile, in May 1960, Martin Luther King Jr. had been acquitted by an all-white jury of the tax evasion charges.) Since this was a civil suit, filed by one citizen seeking repayment of damages inflicted by another party, it was somewhat different from a criminal trial. L. B. Sullivan, who had brought the case before the court, was called the plaintiff, and his lawyers were the plaintiff's lawyers rather than the prosecutors. The *New York Times* and the black ministers were the defendants.

After learning of the New York Times *advertisement, L. B. Sullivan sent registered letters to the newspaper and the four ministers, demanding a retraction of what he considered the "false and defamatory" statements about him in the ad. The* Times *claimed the ad did not refer to him. The ministers, whose names had been listed in the ad without their knowledge, did not respond.*

THE CASE FOR THE PLAINTIFF

M. Roland Nachman and his team of attorneys who represented the plaintiff challenged the truth of a number of statements in the ad. One of its sections stated that King had been arrested seven times. Another part of the ad read as follows:

> In Montgomery, Alabama, after students sang "My Country, 'Tis of Thee" on the State Capitol steps, their leaders were expelled from school, and truckloads of police armed with shotguns and tear-gas ringed the Alabama State College Campus. When the entire student body protested to state authorities, . . . their dining hall was padlocked in an attempt to starve them into submission.

The attorneys for the plaintiff presented evidence that King had been arrested only four times, that the students had actually sung "The Star-Spangled Banner," and that the university had expelled the students because they had attempted to integrate the lunch counter at the Montgomery County courthouse.

The plaintiff's attorneys argued that the advertisement's purpose was to tear down the reputation of the South's elected leaders, giving as an example the following statement from the ad: "Again and again, the Southern violators have answered Dr. King's peaceful protests with intimidation and violence." The full-page ad also claimed that civil rights workers were "being met with an unprecedented wave of terror."

Although the ad did not mention L. B. Sullivan or his official government office by name, it did name the city of Montgomery and its police force and, therefore, his lawyers argued, Sullivan's reputation had clearly been injured. The attorneys maintained that by listing two

M. Roland Nachman later would become president of the Alabama State Bar and often gave lectures on the controversial Sullivan case.

black Montgomery pastors as sponsors, the ad had aimed its unfair accusations at the city.

The plaintiff's lawyers further pointed out that the ad referred to police acting in an unjust and racist manner. Since one of Sullivan's primary duties as commissioner was to oversee the Montgomery police, he believed that the ad clearly reproached his "ability and integrity."

Sullivan's lawyers then called on Grover Cleveland Hall Jr., editor of the Montgomery *Advertiser*, to support the claim that the *New York Times* ad had targeted Sullivan. Although Hall and Sullivan were not on good terms because of disagreements over certain *Advertiser* articles, the editor was willing to testify on Sullivan's behalf. Hall said that when he read the advertisement, he assumed it was criticizing Sullivan.

Five other witnesses testified that they, too, associated statements in the ad with Sullivan. Although none of them believed the ad's allegations of injustice, they all said that had they not already known the true situation surrounding the events described in the advertisement, the ad would have made them think less of Sullivan.

Nachman urged the jury to find the defendants guilty of libel in order to deter them "from doing such a thing again" and to deter others from using newspapers to destroy the reputations of government officials. Robert E. Steiner from the plaintiff's team of lawyers argued that the only way to get large news organizations to act responsibly was "to hit them in the pocketbook."

THE CASE FOR THE DEFENSE

Representing the *New York Times*, T. Eric Embry argued that the court should dismiss the charges because nothing in the ad "even remotely" referred to Sullivan. Harding Bancroft, an executive at the *Times*, confirmed that no one connected with the paper thought that any of the language in the ad referred to Sullivan.

Embry got the plaintiff's witnesses to concede that they thought no worse of Sullivan after reading the advertisement. In fact, four of the witnesses had never even seen the advertisement until Sullivan's lawyers called it to their attention. The *Times* had such a small circulation in Alabama—fewer than 400 subscribers in the entire state, and only 35 in Montgomery—that the advertisement could have had little effect on Sullivan's reputation. Given

*T. Eric Embry,
the only Alabama
lawyer the* New
York Times
*could find to
represent them,
became a justice
on the Alabama
State Supreme
Court in 1975.*

that no one in the city of Montgomery had voiced any criticism of Sullivan as a result of the ad, Embry asked, "Where is the evidence that has shown you that Mr. Sullivan suffered any injury?"

Embry also disputed the plaintiff's claim that the ad was full of malicious lies and that the *Times* had known many of its statements were false. The attorney pointed out that King's supporters had been under a tight deadline to raise money for King's defense. Under those circumstances, Embry said, the information in the ad was quite accurate. Its only substantial error—claiming that college officials had padlocked the dining hall to starve protesting students—hurt the reputation of the college, not Sullivan. Therefore, the court could not possibly view that statement as being critical of Sullivan.

Finally, the defendant's attorney pointed out that the First Amendment to the U.S. Constitution guarantees the freedom of the press to criticize public officials.

Fred Gray and several associates represented the black ministers whom Sullivan had charged in the libel suit. These lawyers argued that the ministers knew nothing about the advertisement and did not authorize the use of their names in it. John Murray, who had helped to write the copy for the ad, supported their claim. He admitted that the people responsible for the ad had included the pastors' names without consulting them. The writers had justified their decision by saying that because the black ministers were part of the overall civil rights movement, they would probably have given their support to the advertisement.

LEGAL ISSUES

The libel laws for the state of Alabama allow public officials to collect money in a civil case from those who wrong them. But this can happen only if a defendant criticizes a government agency under the plaintiff's supervision in a way that would "injure him in his reputation" or bring "him into public contempt as an official." Although the plaintiff has to prove that the defendant published harmful or insulting statements, Alabama laws put the burden of proof on the defense.

Judge Walter Burgwyn Jones told the jury that according to Alabama's libel laws, several statements in the *New York Times* ad were libelous and harmful to the reputation of anyone to whom they referred.

If the criticisms were true, the jury could not consider them libel. But under Alabama civil law, the court presumed such statements to be false unless the defendant proved them true. The *Times*, Judge Jones said, had made no attempt to prove the truth of the statements in the ad. In fact, the newspaper even admitted that some of the statements were not true. Therefore, the judge explained, the jury had only two issues to consider in deciding responsibility for damages, or *liability*. First, did the defendants publish the ad? Second, did the statements in the ad concern L. B. Sullivan?

YOU ARE THE JUROR.
WHAT IS YOUR DECISION?

What verdict do you declare in the libel charges against the *New York Times* and the ministers?

Option 1	**Neither the ministers nor the *Times* is liable for these charges.**
Option 2	**The ministers are not liable, but the *Times* is liable.**
Option 3	**Both the ministers and the *Times* are liable.**

Harding Bancroft testified for the New York Times. *His newspaper faced $3 million in libel suits from Sullivan and other officials due to the "Heed Their Rising Voices" ad.*

*Fred Shuttlesworth (left) and Ralph Abernathy (center),
two of the defendants in the Sullivan case, march with
Martin Luther King Jr. in April 1963 in downtown
Birmingham, Alabama, to protest segregation in
Birmingham businesses. Soon after the photograph was
taken, the three men were arrested for defying a court
order not to march in demonstrations.*

**The jurors chose *Option 3*. They found all of the
defendants liable for the charges.**

An all-white jury took only 2 hours and 20 minutes
to reach a decision against the ministers and the *New York
Times*. It recommended that the defendants pay Sullivan
the entire amount of the suit—$500,000.

ANALYSIS

The jury in this case was under tremendous pressure from
the local community. The trial took place in an atmosphere of intense discrimination against blacks and against
those who supported the civil rights movement. Seating

in the courtroom was segregated. The *Alabama Journal* published a front-page photograph of the jurors along with their names so that everyone in Montgomery would know who they were. Of the 36 prospective jurors, only 2 were black—and the plaintiff's lawyers rejected them from serving on the jury.

As an immediate result of the verdict, the state seized and sold land and an automobile belonging to Ralph Abernathy—one of the ministers charged in the case—to pay off part of the damages awarded to Sullivan. The judgment also threatened to ruin perhaps the most influential newspaper in the United States. As one expert observed, if the *New York Times* had to pay the damages awarded by the court in this and other lawsuits filed by Alabama officials, "there was a reasonable question of whether the *Times* . . . could survive."

The governor of Alabama and other state officials followed L. B. Sullivan's example and sued for libel in separate cases which totaled almost $300 million in damage claims. All over the South, authorities now used the threat of libel charges to make it risky for the national press to report on civil rights struggles.

Aware of the historical and personal significance of Sullivan's judgment, the defendants appealed the case to the Alabama Supreme Court, pointing out the lack of references to L. B. Sullivan and stating that the lower court's decision violated the defendants' right to freedom of expression. But on August 30, 1962, that court upheld the verdict, declaring that "the first Amendment of the U.S. Constitution does not protect libelous publications."

The defendants appealed yet again—this time to the highest court in the nation, the U.S. Supreme Court. Triumph finally came on March 9, 1964, when the Supreme Court unanimously reversed the Alabama court's

Going beyond usual Supreme Court practice in the Sullivan case, Justice William Brennan reexamined the evidence and ruled it was insufficient to find the New York Times *and the ministers guilty of libel.*

ruling. In the decision, Justice William Brennan wrote that "the pall of fear and timidity imposed upon those who would give voice to public criticism is an atmosphere in which the First Amendment freedoms cannot survive."

Speaking for the Court, Justice Brennan argued that in order to limit the powers of the state and maintain the government's accountability to the people, neither speech nor writing that criticized either the government or its officials could be suppressed only because it contained damaging assessments of official actions.

In this historic case, the U.S. Supreme Court set a standard that has since protected freedom of the press in the United States. As a result of the Sullivan ruling, unless a plaintiff in a suit can prove that a defendant wrote

Fred Gray, the attorney who defended the four black ministers, became a partner in a Tuskegee, Alabama, law firm. He is also the author of Bus Ride to Justice, *a book about the civil rights movement that includes a chapter on the Sullivan case.*

falsehoods with *malice*—that is, with deliberateness or recklessness—then criticism of public officials is legal, even when the criticism was undeserved or untrue.

This case again demonstrated the difficult task that jurors face. Although they followed the Alabama judge's instructions about the case's legal matters, they ended up reaching a decision that, according to the unanimous decision of the nine justices of the U.S. Supreme Court, violated the law of the land.

3

THE CHICAGO SEVEN
CONVENTION RIOTS
1969

Political passions in the United States have seldom run deeper than during the 1968 presidential campaign. In the months leading up to the election, assassins gunned down both civil rights leader Martin Luther King Jr. and presidential candidate Robert F. Kennedy. Americans are deeply split over the U.S. government's foreign policy. Although Congress never declared war on the North Vietnamese, half a million American soldiers have been sent to fight against the Communist government of North Vietnam and defend the unpopular military regime of South Vietnam.

Opponents of the Vietnam War were optimistic when President Lyndon B. Johnson, who had authorized the use of U.S. troops and had escalated the nation's involvement in the conflict, decided not to run for reelection in 1968. But their hopes sank again when Johnson's

The June 6, 1968, death of Robert F. Kennedy, the front-running liberal Democrat who opposed the war, shocked followers who had hoped to work within the political system to bring back U.S. troops from Vietnam.

vice-president, Hubert H. Humphrey, who supported the administration's policy, grabbed a strong lead in the race for the Democratic Party's presidential nomination.

In August 1968, many antiwar protesters traveled to the Democratic National Convention in Chicago. When city officials turned down their request for permits to march and to hold rallies, more than 3,000 protesters gathered in Lincoln Park, believing that the city was denying them their right to free speech. Chicago police attacked the demonstrators with clubs and tear gas when they refused to disband.

Hearing about these incidents, as many as 20,000 antiwar protesters, most of them young people, joined the demonstration. Some taunted the police, which provoked more attacks. Television-news crews beamed clips of the violence across the nation.

Congress had recently passed antiriot legislation that sought to prevent outside agitators from coming into a community to stir up trouble. But, fearing the law was unconstitutional, President Johnson's Department of Justice declined to prosecute the protesters. Then, in November 1968, Richard M. Nixon won the presidential election, and his administration brought charges against eight leaders of the various protest groups. The U.S. government charged the eight with "conspiracy to travel across state lines for the purpose of causing a riot."

On September 24, 1969, the trial against the eight protest leaders began in a federal district court in downtown Chicago. When Judge Julius J. Hoffman refused to

To the young demonstrators in Chicago, President Johnson's meetings with advisors over Vietnam strategy amounted to war games played with their lives.

allow defendant Bobby Seale to act as his own attorney, the first phase of the trial erupted into chaos. Because repeated protests by Seale and others had disrupted the court proceedings, Hoffman declared a mistrial in Seale's case. The trial continued with only seven defendants— Jerry Rubin, Abbie Hoffman, John Froines, Lee Weiner, David Dellinger, Rennie Davis, and Tom Hayden.

Bobby Seale, leader of the Black Panthers (lower left), and the other defendants: (top row, left to right) Jerry Rubin and Abbie Hoffman, cofounders of the Youth International Party; Tom Hayden and Rennie Davis, two founders of Students for a Democratic Society; (bottom row, second from left to right) Lee Weiner, John Froines, and David Dellinger.

THE CASE FOR THE PROSECUTION

Thomas Foran, a U.S. attorney for the state of Illinois, and a team of lawyers, presented the government's case. Foran described the defendants as "evil men" who intended to cause violent protests in Chicago, arranging for others to come and inciting the new arrivals to riot. A total of 53 witnesses testified about the defendants' statements and speeches. According to the prosecutors, their speeches had prompted thousands of young people to come to Chicago and participate in a riot.

David Stahl, a Chicago deputy mayor, testified that the city refused to give the protesters permits to assemble because officials had evidence that the young people were dangerous and were planning to wreck the city. Next, a long series of undercover police and paid informants came to the stand to incriminate the defendants.

One witness said Jerry Rubin had flipped a lighted cigarette at the police and urged others to do the same. Another said Rubin threw a bottle at the police and called for young people in Lincoln Park to arm themselves. Yet another witness for the prosecution reported that Rubin predicted the police would be provoked to violence.

Police undercover agents reported that Abbie Hoffman told the protesters to storm the Hilton Hotel, site of some of the worst violence during the convention. To prove that Hoffman was dangerous, the prosecution presented a transcript of a speech he had made a year after the riots, giving instruction on making "Molotov cocktails," a type of homemade bomb. The prosecution also presented the tape of an interview that Hoffman had granted during the week of the convention, in which he said the police "care more about a City Ordinance than they do about the destruction of Chicago." According to the prosecution, Hoffman's taped statement indicated that he and his cohorts intended to destroy the city in retaliation for the refusal of city officials to grant the protesters permits to march and hold rallies.

An FBI informant quoted Tom Hayden as saying in a speech given a month before the convention that people "must be ready to shed their blood." Another infiltrator of the antiwar movement reported that those who knew Hayden well considered him to be a violent person.

A young student undercover agent testified that Rennie Davis told his supporters that rally organizers would use rock music to "lure" the young people to Lincoln Park, where they would then riot. The prosecution cited a speech Davis made after the convention in which he urged young people to become "part of a growing force for insurrection in the United States." According to the prosecution, recruiting people for *insurrection*, or the overthrow of the government, was clearly the kind of activity targeted by the federal antiriot law.

One undercover witness testified that he saw John Froines throw rocks during the riot and heard David Dellinger say he led a peaceful assembly as a "diversion" to distract the attention of police officers from the main group of protesters. According to witnesses, the protest organizers recruited experts in the martial arts to instruct marchers on how to fight the police. Prior to the protest, the Chicago Seven repeatedly used obscene language and showed utter contempt for the U.S. government.

According to chief prosecutor Foran, all of this testimony proved that the defendants had come to Chicago with the intention of provoking the disorder that had marred the week of the Democratic National Convention. The protest was part of their master plan to defy the law and the government of the United States.

Thomas Foran (left) laid out the prosecution's case. Defense attorneys William Kunstler (center) and Leonard Weinglass clashed with the judge and would request a mistrial because their mail had been opened, their offices searched, and their clients wiretapped.

THE CASE FOR THE DEFENSE

Attorneys William Kunstler and Leonard Weinglass prepared the case for the seven defendants, arguing that they were merely asserting their First Amendment rights of assembly and free speech. Many witnesses, including poet Allen Ginsberg and folk singer Pete Seeger, testified that the protest groups were peaceful. The protesters came to Chicago not to cause violence but to demonstrate against what they believed to be an illegal and immoral war in Vietnam and to decry racism and poverty in the United States.

According to defense witnesses, protest leaders had gone out of their way to cooperate with Chicago officials. The Chicago Seven had made a determined effort to work within the system by attempting to obtain permits to march and hold rallies, but the authorities had rejected their requests. Defense witnesses admitted that the protest leaders taught martial-arts techniques to their followers. But, they insisted, the leaders had instructed the protesters to use these techniques only in self-defense.

The defendants' legal team maintained that the U.S. government was prosecuting the seven because of their radical political beliefs. Attorneys Kunstler and Weinglass argued that the government's actions illegally violated the constitutional protection of the free expression of political beliefs, however unpopular they may be.

The defense then argued that the police, not the demonstrators, had created most of the violence during the Chicago convention and that the trial was simply a public-relations ploy to try to shift blame for the riots from the police to the demonstrators. The defense cited independent reports that blamed the convention riots on police overreacting against the small minority of protesters who had tried to provoke them.

As evidence, the defense lawyers produced a police officer's report about one of the riot sites. In it, he stated that the "frontal attack and release of gas" caused a "complete collapse of order." According to this report, the marchers behaved well until the police attacked them.

Many witnesses for the defense testified to acts of police brutality. Famed author Norman Mailer said the police had "systematically" beaten protesters. The defense reinforced that argument by showing a photograph of police throwing a woman over the railing of an underground parking garage and a film in which members of the National Guard threatened a woman who was driving with a carful of young children in the area.

The defense next produced an undercover agent who was present when Davis supposedly said he was using rock music to lure young people to Lincoln Park. The

Enraged that the protesters were mocking the political process—they nominated a pig for president!—Chicago mayor Richard Daley ordered the police to end the disruptions outside the Democratic National Convention.

agent said he had heard no such comment and had seen no violence or any attempt to incite violence on the part of the defendants. Even witnesses for the prosecution admitted to never seeing any of the defendants carrying a weapon. A Chicago police supervisor on the scene testified that Abbie Hoffman had been polite and that violence erupted only when the police attacked.

According to the defense, the charges of conspiracy were absurd. The seven defendants hardly knew each other. They lived in different states, led different organizations whose goals and methods were often far apart, and certainly had never met together to plan a riot. In the words of defendant Abbie Hoffman, "We couldn't agree on lunch." How could these defendants manage to conspire to pull off something on such a huge scale as the

Chicago riots? Furthermore, even the prosecution characterized the riots as "spontaneous acts of violence." "How do you plan spontaneous acts of violence?" Abbie Hoffman asked the court.

Lawyers for the defense then cast doubt on the testimony of the prosecution's witnesses, noting that virtually all of them worked for the U.S. government. One even received a promotion right after giving damaging testimony about the defendants! The attorneys for the Chicago Seven pointed out that U.S. government officials were pressuring the prosecution witnesses to back their version of the events. Thousands of bystanders had witnessed what had happened outside the convention center. Yet the prosecution team had called only undercover police, agents of the government, and paid informants to support its story. Why hadn't prosecutors brought to the witness stand some of the ordinary citizens who had been on the streets during the riots?

Furthermore, much of the testimony that prosecution witnesses provided at the trial was different from what the same witnesses had given at a grand-jury hearing to decide whether the case should come to trial. Why had they changed their testimony?

Witnesses for the defense testified that Jerry Rubin had become ill and was not even present at the demonstration on August 25, the date prosecution witnesses claimed he had been inciting riots.

Attorney Weinglass explained the defendants' often shocking language by saying they shared a passionate commitment to peace and justice. "Men of strong convictions," he intoned, "use strong language." The defense criticized the U.S. government for trying to imprison men simply for speaking what the government considered to be dangerous views. Kunstler reinforced Weinglass's point, arguing that "the right of men to speak boldly, to live and die free" depended on the jury's decision.

Defense attorney Weinglass furthermore reminded the jurors that the government had not been able to bring forward as evidence a single recording, photograph, or any other kind of proof of any incitement to riot. He pointed out that the only kind of speech the First Amendment to the Constitution does not allow is speech that creates an immediate danger. Anything the defendants said a year before or a year after the Chicago demonstrations would not fall into that category.

THE PROSECUTION'S REBUTTAL

To refute the defense claim that the riots resulted from an unprovoked attack by the police, the prosecution produced a number of witnesses. One Chicago newspaper reporter described how demonstrators had pelted police with a barrage of bottles.

During the trial, the defendants had often mocked Judge Julius Hoffman—making comments out of order, cracking jokes, blowing kisses to the jury, and shouting out crude remarks. Attorney Foran told jurors that this type of behavior demonstrated that the defendants were lawless, arrogant, uncivilized people who took pleasure in demeaning the most sacred institutions of the United States and inciting others to do the same.

LEGAL ISSUES

The law allowed the jury to find some of the defendants guilty and others not guilty. In order to prove conspiracy, the government had to prove beyond a reasonable doubt that two or more persons had planned and carried out at least one step toward committing a crime. Judge Hoffman loosened this requirement by telling jurors that in a charge of conspiracy, "the substance of the crime was a state of mind" rather than any specific act.

The incitement charge accused the defendants of traveling to a state "with intent to incite, . . . organize, promote, encourage, participate in, or carry on a riot." Judge Hoffman said the law distinguishes between advocating violence (supporting violence in certain situations) and inciting others to violence (directly encouraging others to commit an immediate act of violence). The judge pointed out that the First Amendment protects the freedom to advocate violence, but not to incite violence.

Judge Hoffman explained to the jury that if others had committed illegal acts that a defendant had encouraged, then the defendant was as guilty as he would be if he had committed the acts himself. In determining whether the defendants had intended to incite violence at the Chicago convention, the jurors could take into account the defendants' courtroom conduct and actions since the convention.

Finally, Judge Hoffman declared that "the jury cannot question the wisdom of any rule of law; it can only decide the facts." So even if jurors felt the defendants' acts were justified, they must find the defendants guilty if those acts violated the law.

YOU ARE THE JUROR.
WHAT IS YOUR DECISION?

The past five months of the trial have been bizarre. Judge Hoffman has ranted in court and ridiculed the defendants and their lawyers—even deliberately mispronouncing the name of one of the defense attorneys. His behavior has been nearly as outlandish as the defendants' antics. Now you have to sift through all of this absurdity and come to a decision. Keep in mind that you must judge the defendants individually and may find some guilty and some not guilty. What verdict do you declare in the case of the Chicago Seven?

Option 1　　**The Chicago Seven are not guilty of conspiracy and incitement charges.**

Option 2　　**The Chicago Seven are guilty on both charges.**

Option 3　　**The Chicago Seven are not guilty of conspiracy, but they are guilty of incitement to riot.**

Option 4　　**The Chicago Seven are guilty of conspiracy, but they are not guilty of incitement to riot.**

Before their trial, Abbie Hoffman speaks at a New York City rally for the Chicago Eight while the other defendants stand with him (left to right): Tom Hayden, John Froines, Jerry Rubin, Bobby Seale, David Dellinger, Rennie Davis, and Lee Weiner.

The jurors chose *Option 3*. They found all seven defendants not guilty of conspiracy but found five of them guilty of incitement to riot.

The jury began deliberations on February 14, 1970, four days after the trial ended. The jury of 10 women and 2 men—all but one of them middle-aged and all middle class—was sharply divided on all the issues. On their first ballot, 8 favored conviction on all counts and 4 voted for acquittal on all counts. Even after long days of arguing, few of the jurors changed their minds.

Because of this impasse, the jurors twice sent notes to Judge Hoffman, saying they were unable to reach a unanimous verdict. When jurors cannot come to a unanimous decision, they are a *hung jury*, and the prosecution must retry the case with a new jury or set the defendants free. But Judge Hoffman did not respond to the messages, so the jurors were forced to continue deliberating.

After four days, the jury reached a compromise. On February 18, 1970, it declared all defendants not guilty of conspiracy, and Lee Weiner and John Froines not guilty on all charges. The jury found the other five defendants guilty of crossing state lines to incite a riot.

Judge Hoffman sentenced each of those found guilty of incitement to the maximum sentence—five years in prison and a $5,000 fine, plus the costs of prosecution. In addition, he imposed jail sentences—ranging from two months to more than four years—on several of the defendants and their lawyers for *contempt of court*, or disrespect for the judicial process.

ANALYSIS

The American Civil Liberties Union (ACLU) called the Chicago Seven case "probably the most important political trial in the history of the United States." Those who called the trial "political" rather than "criminal" believed that officials of the United States government were attempting to punish individuals simply for exercising their guaranteed right to express their opinions. The ACLU and others saw a victory for the prosecution as a green light for the government to continue to violate the rights of its citizens.

The fact that the prosecution's witnesses included dozens of agents who had infiltrated political groups that opposed U.S. policy created the impression that the government was trying to silence its critics. One juror, Shirley Seaholm, admitted that for "the first time I was afraid of our government."

Bolstering this view was the fact that mail belonging to defense attorneys had been opened by the court. In addition, their offices had been searched and the government had illegally wiretapped the defendants' telephones. Defense attorneys cited these abuses of power in their argument for a mistrial.

On the other hand, many Americans and several jurors believed that the government's actions were proper. They thought the defendants were dangerous people who had abused the rights of free speech in an effort to destroy the United States. Their prosecution was justified to maintain law and order.

The compromise verdict satisfied almost no one, including the jurors. Even as the jury foreman was reading the verdict, one juror who had originally voted for acquittal on all counts was regretting her decision to agree

After Judge Hoffman handed down the contempt sentences, 3,000 people rallied in New York City to show the judge what they thought of his demand for respect in the courtroom.

to the compromise. "I voted five men guilty on . . . speeches I don't remember," she thought, breaking into tears.

Much of the fault with the compromise verdict lay with the judge. Judge Hoffman gave jurors the distinct impression that he would not accept a hung jury and that he would keep the jurors locked in a room until they agreed on a verdict. The jury members were not aware that a judge could not legally subject them to this kind of treatment.

In fact, Judge Hoffman's strange conduct and obvious bias against the defendants during the trial prompted a court of appeals to throw out the verdicts and order a new trial for the five convicted defendants. Declining to try the case again, the government released them all. The government, however, did try the defendants and their lawyers for contempt of court. In 1972, William Kunstler, David Dellinger, Jerry Rubin, and Abbie Hoffman were found guilty of contempt charges, but they were given suspended sentences and did not serve time in jail.

4

PATTY HEARST
VICTIM OR OUTLAW?
1976

On the night of February 4, 1974, members of a radical political group called the Symbionese Liberation Army (SLA) broke into Patty Hearst's apartment in Berkeley, California, and dragged the screaming young woman into the darkness. Most people assumed that the kidnappers were holding Hearst, the daughter of wealthy newspaper publisher Randolph Hearst, for ransom. Indeed, in the days after the kidnapping, the SLA first sought a "prisoner exchange" for two jailed SLA members. When that failed, they demanded that Hearst's father finance the defense of two jailed SLA members and fund a program to feed all the poor people in California.

But two months later, on April 15, 1974, Hearst suddenly surfaced during a robbery of a branch of the Hibernia Bank in San Francisco. Hearst held a sawed-off shotgun and stood guard while other members of the SLA grabbed the money. Captured on film by the bank's hidden camera, Hearst appeared to take an active part in the robbery.

On May 16, Hearst sprayed automatic-rifle fire at a sporting-goods store in Los Angeles to cover the escape of SLA members William and Emily Harris, who were allegedly shoplifting. The next day, Los Angeles police trapped most of the SLA members in a house. Six of them died in the exchange of gunfire that followed, but Hearst was not among them.

Following the shootout, police tracked Hearst across the country for 16 months but never caught up with her. Finally, on September 18, 1975, she was found in San Francisco, and federal law-enforcement officials arrested her and charged her with armed robbery. Patty Hearst's strange trial began in San Francisco's Federal Court building on February 4, 1976.

THE CASE FOR THE PROSECUTION

The prosecutor, U.S. Attorney James Browning, conceded that the SLA had kidnapped Patty Hearst. But according to Browning, Hearst sympathized with the political aims of her captors and became a willing member of the group. Browning maintained that Hearst freely had taken part in the April 15 Hibernia Bank robbery.

To demonstrate Hearst's sympathy for the SLA, Browning submitted a tape authorities had made of a conversation between Hearst and a friend who had visited her in jail. On the tape, Hearst said she was upset the police had found her. Police reported that when she was captured, Hearst defiantly listed her occupation as "unemployed urban guerrilla."

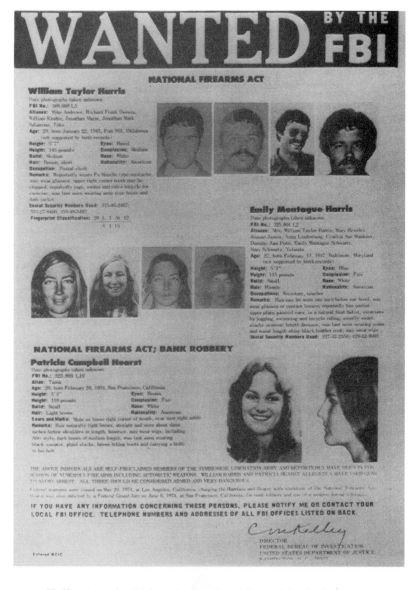

Following the Hibernia Bank robbery, in which two people were shot and over $10,000 was stolen, the FBI named Patricia Hearst a "very dangerous" fugitive for this and other crimes she committed with the SLA.

Hearst's captors told her to identify herself at the Hibernia Bank and make a statement that the group was taking funds for the revolution. Terrified, she managed only to shout her name.

Dr. Joel Fort, a physician who had questioned Hearst in preparation for the trial, testified that she not only had been an active SLA member, but she had also risen in its ranks until she was "queen of the army."

The prosecution introduced documents that investigators found in the apartment Hearst had shared with William and Emily Harris. Those documents included names of banks, a floor plan of a bank, and notes in Hearst's handwriting on how to rob a bank.

According to Browning, the May 16 incident in Los Angeles clearly demonstrated that Hearst had acted of her own free will. Witnesses saw her standing alone in a van outside of the sporting-goods store while the Harrises were inside. Hearst rescued them when they ran into trouble by shooting off bursts of gunfire.

Thomas Dean Matthews, a 19-year-old whom the SLA had taken hostage during their brief spree of terror, testified that he had heard Hearst speak with pride about her role in the SLA's guerrilla war against society. The prosecution also presented evidence that Hearst, using her SLA nickname, Tania, frequently repeated the SLA's revolutionary slogans in her communications.

During the trial, Browning introduced evidence that the SLA had split its bank haul of $10,690 nine ways, and Hearst had received a full share. The prosecutor asked the jury to consider whether the SLA would have included Hearst had she not been a trusted and valued member of their group.

James Browning addresses the jury in this drawing by courtroom artist Rosalie Ritz. In response to public suspicion that the government would not charge a rich heiress with bank robbery, Browning, who was chief U.S. attorney for northern California, announced he would prosecute the case against Patty Hearst himself.

When Hearst took the witness stand, Browning zeroed in on the 16 months she was on the run from the authorities and asked her 42 questions about her activities during that time. Hearst refused to answer every question on the grounds that her reply might tend to incriminate her and "cause danger" to herself and her family. Browning then asked the jury to consider why a hostage, once freed from her captors, would run from the police and refuse to tell anyone what had occurred during her disappearance.

The prosecutor described Hearst as a "rebel in search of a cause." As a teenager, he noted, she had attended five schools in six years and discipline problems had played a large role in her school transfers. Browning asked the jurors not to get bogged down in the jumble of psychological analysis that the defense would present but to judge the case on the facts.

Hearst herself had admitted that she had "acted as a soldier in the people's army." He reminded the jury that Hearst occasionally had been armed when other SLA members were not. The idea of a poor hostage standing armed guard over her captives was "just too big a pill to swallow," he maintained.

THE CASE FOR THE DEFENSE

Nationally known attorney F. Lee Bailey argued in Hearst's defense and put his client on the stand to tell the story of her kidnapping. According to Hearst, her SLA captors had seized her at gunpoint and repeatedly told her they would kill her if she made one false move.

The captors had tied her up, blindfolded her, and stuffed her in a closet for 57 days. During that time, Hearst was raped and deprived of sleep. When they

Before taking on Patty Hearst's defense, F. Lee Bailey had won longshot acquittals in such famous cases as Dr. Sam Sheppard's trial for murdering his wife and Marine captain Ernest Medina's trial for his role in the My Lai massacre in Vietnam.

finally let her out of the closet, the SLA indoctrinated her and made her believe their group was part of a powerful nationwide revolution that was taking over America.

Hearst claimed her captors forced her to participate in the Hibernia Bank robbery and threatened her with violence if she did not cooperate fully. She maintained that she was just a prop and had no ammunition in her gun. Following the crime, the SLA told Hearst that because she had been at the scene with a gun, the U.S. government would consider her a criminal and guilty of bank robbery.

Hearst testified that when she heard this, she felt trapped. Having nowhere to turn, she cooperated with her SLA captors simply to save her life. But, Hearst maintained, she never liked or became friends with them. She claimed to have made an incriminating statement in jail because Emily Harris was in the next cell and could hear what Hearst was saying. Even while in jail, Hearst had feared for her life.

Dr. Louis West, chair of the psychiatry department at UCLA, testified that Hearst was telling the truth. West maintained that Patty Hearst was traumatized by being wrenched from a pampered, sheltered life into a violent, life-threatening, and often sleep-deprived situation. The psychologist said that during Hearst's time with the SLA, her IQ had dropped from around 130 to 109. The experience had so devastated her that she still trembled at the mention of her kidnapping, William or Emily Harris, or her imprisonment in the closet.

During his testing, Dr. West had discovered that Hearst had much in common with prisoners of war who had been interrogated by their captors. (An expert on the brainwashing of hostages, West had examined 59 U.S. Air Force officers captured and tortured by the North Koreans during the Korean War.) He found no evidence that Hearst believed any of the SLA phrases she had used, nor that she believed in any of the actions she had undertaken on behalf of the SLA. "It was a case of be accepted or be killed," West said.

In his testimony, the psychologist insisted that the level of intimidation under which Hearst had lived had made her carry out SLA wishes even when she appeared to be in no danger. She always performed as her captors had conditioned her to perform. When the police brought Hearst into custody, she made a clenched-fist salute. West explained this action and her declaration that she was an unemployed urban guerrilla as classic "survivor's syndrome." She had continued to act as instructed by her captors until she was sure of her safety.

Another brainwashing expert, Dr. Robert Jay Lifton of Yale University, agreed with West. "If one's captors are sufficiently determined and motivated," said Lifton, "they can break down anyone."

Next, the defense called Dr. Martin Orne, a University of Pennsylvania psychiatry professor, to the witness stand. Orne specialized in determining whether or not people were trying to deceive interviewers. In his testimony, Orne stated that when he questioned Hearst before the trial, she "simply did not lie," even when he tried to coax her into doing so.

To counter the prosecution's claims about Hearst's psychological health, Dr. James Stubblebine, a San Francisco psychiatrist, said that the prosecution's expert witness, Dr. Joel Fort, had a reputation among psychologists as an unreliable witness.

Patty Hearst's parents then took the stand and contradicted the prosecutor's image of their daughter. She had not been a wild, rebellious teenager with discipline problems; instead, she was a fun-loving, intelligent, and affectionate person who was close to her family.

Defense attorney Bailey summed up his case by saying that the only clear-cut facts of the case were that the SLA had kidnapped Patty Hearst, intimidated her, and forced her to take part in the April 15 robbery at the Hibernia Bank. Since her arrest, Bailey added, the intimidation had continued. Patty Hearst's parents had been threatened and their home bombed.

Bailey did not deny that Hearst had taken part in the robbery of which she was accused. But, Bailey told the jury, "The question you are here to answer, is: Why? And would you have done the same thing to survive?" He concluded that anyone on the jury also would have followed the kidnappers' orders out of fear. Bailey urged jury members to have compassion for the tiny, frail, ill young woman who was not the criminal in the case, but the victim.

THE PROSECUTOR'S REBUTTAL

In response to some of the defense's claims, James Browning presented additional evidence. West, a psychologist who had testified for the defense, had claimed that Hearst's mental condition had been weakened because her SLA captors deprived her of sleep. But, Browning said, West's report stated that only once in her captivity did her captors wake her during the night.

Browning called on Zigurd Berzins, an eyewitness of the bank robbery, to counter Hearst's claim that she had no ammunition during the Hibernia Bank robbery. Berzins testified that Hearst had two clips of ammunition at the bank.

Finally, Browning attacked Hearst's claim that she had detested her captors, particularly a man named Willie Wolfe, whom she accused of raping her. He produced testimony that Wolfe had given Hearst a gift of a small monkey face carved in stone. Many months after Wolfe's death in the Los Angeles shootout, police found Hearst still carrying the memento.

LEGAL ISSUES

Judge Oliver Carter explained to the jurors that they could legally excuse a person accused of committing a crime if that person had been physically forced to commit the crime or had committed it under threat of violence. But he cautioned that the threat or force "must be present and immediate, . . . a well-founded fear of death or bodily injury with no possible escape from compulsion."

Judge Oliver Carter, shown in this courtroom drawing with attorneys Bailey (left) and Browning, highlighted the crucial question in the trial in his instructions to the jurors: Did they or did they not believe Hearst's testimony about her experience?

YOU ARE THE JUROR.
WHAT IS YOUR DECISION?

You must decide whether Patty Hearst was a victim or a criminal. What verdict do you declare in the charge against her of armed robbery?

Option 1   **Hearst is not guilty.**

Option 2   **Hearst is guilty.**

Before her kidnapping, Patty Hearst was a college student from a loving family. Now she is on trial for a major felony.

Jurors cast their votes three times before the last holdout for acquittal changed his vote to guilty. The lone alternate juror stated that she would not have agreed to convict; thus, the case would have resulted in a hung jury.

The jurors chose *Option 2*. They decided that Patty Hearst was guilty.

After eight weeks of testimony, on March 19, 1976, a San Francisco jury of seven women and five men began their deliberation. It took the jurors—who had been sequestered for the length of the trial—only 12 hours to find Hearst guilty. The jurors later said they believed the defendant was lying about several incidents. Her refusal to testify about her year on the run from the police hurt her case, as did possessing the stone monkey face from Willie Wolfe.

Judge Carter died from a heart attack before pronouncing a sentence in the case. On September 24, 1976, the new judge, William Orrick, sentenced Hearst to seven years in prison. Judge Carter had told a friend that he would probably sentence Hearst to about six months in jail. Even the prosecuting attorney had called for a more lenient sentence than Hearst received.

ANALYSIS

Public reaction to the verdict was evenly split. Some thought Hearst was guilty of being a radical terrorist. They considered her a spoiled brat who got less than she deserved because her dad could afford a high-priced lawyer. The verdict outraged others who felt the government was punishing the victim of a terrible crime.

Before he died, Judge Carter declared the verdict to be "well within the evidence." In fact, prior to Hearst's trial, attorneys had never successfully used brainwashing as a defense in a federal case. According to University of Chicago law professor Franklin E. Zimring, Hearst had obviously endured severe stress during the kidnapping, and the stress might have contributed to her criminal behavior. However, he noted after the trial, there was "no room in the law for the advocacy—or the exploration—of the shades of gray" in this case.

Although he had advised his client to plead the Fifth Amendment, F. Lee Bailey believed that Hearst's refusal to answer the 42 questions about her year on the run may have cost her the case. "I can't think of anything that hurt her more," he later said. The verdict disturbed Bailey, who insisted that Patty Hearst "deserved to be convicted about as much as she deserved to be kidnapped." Many lawyers felt that Bailey had failed in his defense by putting Hearst on the stand and allowing *after-conduct evidence*, or evidence that occurred after the incident for which the defendant was being tried, into the trial.

Although the jurors had convicted Hearst, Judge Orrick's harsh sentence of seven years surprised and outraged them. From the beginning, several of the jurors had believed Hearst to be innocent and, after the trial, all of them eventually came to sympathize with Hearst

Patty Hearst's attorneys F. Lee Bailey (right) and Al Johnson leave a hearing a month after Hearst's conviction. Johnson carries a newspaper with the headline banner "Patty Sentenced."

because of her hostage trauma. According to a marshal who had guarded both Hearst and the sequestered jurors, by the first anniversary of the case, "the jurors were virtually unanimous . . . in agreeing that if a vote were taken today, they would find Patty not guilty."

Law-enforcement officials also grew more sympathetic to Hearst's situation. They dropped most of the charges in the Los Angeles sporting-goods store case and sentenced her to five years of probation. The public rallied behind her and President Jimmy Carter eventually agreed to give her a pardon. On February 1, 1979, after serving part of her seven-year term, Patty Hearst was released from prison. The federal government decided not to prosecute her for other crimes of which she had been accused during her days with the SLA.

In the years since she was freed, Patty Hearst has started a family and pursued a career as a writer and actress. (She married her former bodyguard, San Francisco police officer Bernard Shaw, following her release from prison.) In 1982, she published a book about her ordeal, *Every Secret Thing*, but has concentrated on other projects since then. A movie actress, she has appeared in a number of films, including *Crybaby* and *Serial Mom*. In 1996, she published a mystery, *Murder at San Simeon*, which was set in the famous Hearst Castle that her grandfather had built in the 1920s.

5

DAN WHITE
THE TWINKIE DEFENSE
1979

On November 10, 1978, Dan White unexpectedly resigned his elected position as a city supervisor in San Francisco, California. White, a former police officer, had been a key conservative vote on a deeply divided board of supervisors. Four days later, under pressure from those who supported his views, White changed his mind and asked Mayor George Moscone to give him his position back.

Initially, Moscone agreed to White's request. But then the mayor came under fire from those strongly opposed to the reappointment of a man who had thwarted many liberal programs. Harvey Milk, a supervisor who was the first openly homosexual person to be elected as a public official in the United States, provided the strongest opposition to White regaining his seat on the San Francisco Board of Supervisors.

Yielding to political pressure, Moscone changed his mind about reappointing White. On the day Moscone was to announce his decision, Dan White came to city hall and asked to see the mayor. Shortly after their meeting began, White shot and killed Moscone. Minutes later, the former supervisor asked Harvey Milk to meet with him in an empty office. Once they were in the room, White shot Milk to death.

White, a former police officer, turned himself in to his old police friends. He claimed that he had not planned to commit the murders; his mind had simply snapped under unbearable stress. White's lawyers argued that he was guilty only of manslaughter and not of the intentional, preplanned murders with which the state had charged him. Nearly six months later, on May 1, 1979, the closely watched trial began.

The bodies of Mayor George Moscone and Supervisor Harvey Milk are put into an ambulance as a crowd gathers outside San Francisco City Hall.

In 1975, a liberal coalition favoring gay rights and opposing the influence of business interests on politicians elected George Moscone mayor of San Francisco. He had wanted to be mayor of what he called "the world's greatest city" since he was a little boy.

THE CASE FOR THE PROSECUTION

Prosecutor Thomas Norman, a deputy district attorney, used White's confession and brought in witnesses to establish the events that had taken place on the morning of November 27. That day, White had arrived at city hall wearing a gun and carrying extra ammunition. Instead of entering through the front door—where a metal detector would have discovered his weapon—he crawled into the building through a window.

At about 10:30 A.M., White asked to speak with Mayor Moscone. After White had been in the mayor's office for only a few minutes, witnesses heard White shouting. Shortly thereafter, they heard shots. The coroner, Dr. Boyd Stephens, testified that White had wounded

Moscone with his first two bullets. He then carefully fired two more bullets into the mayor's head from about six inches away.

White reloaded his gun, stuck his head into Harvey Milk's office, and asked to speak with Milk. Escorting Milk down the hall, White led him to his old supervisor's office. White fired three times as Milk frantically tried to scramble away. According to the coroner, White then fired the fourth and fifth fatal bullets into the back of Milk's head. Next, witnesses testified, White walked down the hall and dashed out of the building. Less than an hour later, White surrendered to police.

According to the prosecutor, White's action was neither an accident nor a killing that had erupted in the heat of the moment. Instead, it was a clear-cut case of first-degree murder. No matter what White claimed about the incident, Norman pointed out, "Actions speak louder than words."

When the police asked White why he had brought the gun into city hall, his only answer was "I don't know. I just put it on." The prosecution maintained that no one carries a hidden gun and extra ammunition without intending to shoot someone.

Furthermore, asked the prosecutor, why would someone who did not intend to commit murder avoid metal detectors? And how could White claim he had not intended to commit the murders when he had executed his victims in cold blood with precisely aimed, point-blank shots into their skulls? Were these shots not meant to "finish off" the victims? How could White claim he had not intended to commit murder when he paused to reload his weapon after killing Moscone and before he went to see Milk? Dan White's story made no sense, Norman told the jury.

Harvey Milk was hailed by many as "The Mayor of Castro Street," referring to the gay neighborhood where he lived and owned a camera shop. During his short political career, Milk gave hope to thousands of gay people that they would one day have an equal place in society.

THE CASE FOR THE DEFENSE

Defense attorney Douglas Schmidt conceded that White had killed the two men. He also admitted that the facts surrounding the killings were as the prosecution had described them. But, Schmidt insisted, Dan White was a good man, and "good people, fine people with fine backgrounds, simply don't kill people in cold blood."

With that in mind, the defense attorney set out to show that White was indeed an upstanding person. One of the main witnesses to support this view was Officer Frank Falzon, the man who had taken White's confession. Although Falzon was a witness for the prosecution, Falzon observed, under Schmidt's questioning, that in all the years he had known White as a police officer, a softball teammate, and a friend, he had seen White lose his temper only once. White, according to Falzon, was a "man among men." A psychologist confirmed this image by saying White was not capable of deliberately planning a murder or holding such extreme malice against someone that he would seek to commit murder.

The city's new mayor, Dianne Feinstein, who had been selected by the board of supervisors to replace Mayor Moscone, also portrayed White as an honest, idealistic man who had gone into politics to protect what he considered to be traditional American family values. What he perceived as the deceit of some fellow politicians and his own inability to preserve San Francisco as a comfortable place for families to live frustrated him. One witness testified that White would spend hours trying to decide how to vote on an important issue only to discover that his colleagues were making deals that White did not believe were for the good of the city.

Schmidt then outlined the terrible pressure that White had faced in the weeks preceding the crime. Although he worked long hours trying to support his family with his fast-food stand, the Hot Potato, he could not make ends meet and was in danger of losing his home.

Next, a battery of psychiatrists testified that White was suffering from mental as well as financial problems. Reeling under the pressures of his job and his duties as a city supervisor, White stayed up late at night, stuffing himself with Twinkies, doughnuts, potato chips, candy bars, and cola. The consumption of so much junk food had produced what one psychiatrist called a chemical imbalance. That is, White was suffering from extreme fluctuations in his blood-sugar levels, which worsened his existing manic-depression. In this state, his psychiatrists testified, White had a "diminished mental capacity"—he had not been in his right mind when he shot Mayor George Moscone and Supervisor Harvey Milk.

According to his attorney, Dan White had received word the night before the killings that Moscone had gone back on his agreement and would not be reappointing him to his supervisor's post. White then stayed up all night, eating Twinkies and drinking soda pop.

Dr. George Solmon, a psychiatrist who testified for the defense, claimed that on the morning of the murders, White had carried his gun with him as "a security blanket." The defense attorney also noted that White had heard rumors that hit squads from a radical group called the Peoples Temple were lurking in San Francisco and targeting public officials. Defense attorney Schmidt offered this rumor as a valid reason for White to be carrying a weapon. The defense insisted that White entered city hall through a window because he did not know the policeman who was checking for weapons at the front door and did not want to put him in an awkward position by refusing to submit to the metal-detector check.

Up to the point of their meeting on November 27, Moscone had not given White his final decision about his reappointment as a city supervisor. According to White's tape-recorded confession, when he and the mayor met, White asked Moscone if he had decided against the reappointment. The psychiatrists who testified for the defense stated that when he heard the mayor's reply, an immediate biochemical change—brought on by his junk-food binge and the overwhelming pressure he had been experiencing—took place in White's body and made him crack.

As White stood in Moscone's office, he felt a "roaring" in his ears, and then, in what a psychiatrist called an

Defense attorney Doug Schmidt tried to pick a jury that did not like the way the city had changed under the influence of gays and liberals.

"uncontrolled breakthrough of primitive rage," he shot the mayor. The psychiatrist testified that White pulled the trigger because it would have offended his morality to punch an older man in the face.

According to the psychiatrists testifying for the defense, at that point White was operating strictly by instinct. His police training caused him to reload his weapon instinctively. When he then went to speak to Harvey Milk and tried to explain his frustration and desperation, he said Milk smirked at him. Again, White's mind snapped, and he shot Milk with the same uncontrolled rage that had led him to kill Moscone.

Schmidt summed up his argument by saying that "nobody can say that the things that happened to him days or weeks preceding wouldn't make a reasonable and ordinary man at least mad." Sitting blankly throughout the entire court proceedings, White did indeed look like a man who had broken under mental strain.

THE PROSECUTOR'S REBUTTAL

Prosecutor Norman called to the stand a psychologist who had interviewed White shortly after the killings. This man testified that White appeared calm and sane and showed no remorse for his victims. On cross-examination, however, the defense got the psychologist to admit that he had interviewed White on only one occasion and had never seen him again for follow-up interviews.

Countering the claims of mental illness, the prosecutor reminded jurors that, according to the coroner's report, the murders appeared to be cold-blooded executions, not uncontrolled violent outbursts. The attorney for the prosecution noted that White had taken his time and aimed carefully and deliberately with his last bullets to make sure his victims were dead. The fact that he brought extra ammunition with him and reloaded just before going after Harvey Milk, said Norman, destroyed the notion that White had killed Milk in a sudden fit of anger.

LEGAL ISSUES

Judge Walter Calcagno told the jurors that they could find Dan White guilty of one of three charges: first-degree murder, second-degree murder, or voluntary manslaughter.

First-degree murder involves a deliberate and malicious act of killing that is planned ahead of time and then carried out. *Second-degree murder* involves a deliberate act of killing when the murder is not planned in advance. *Voluntary manslaughter* is a killing that occurs in the heat of the moment or when the killer's capacity is diminished. As Douglas Schmidt had suggested, the judge also instructed jurors that one could be provoked to the heat of passion by longstanding events as well as by an immediate incident.

In this case, the state of California could punish first-degree murder with death or life in prison. The two other charges would involve shorter prison sentences. Since the case involved two charges of murder, the jury could find the defendant guilty of different degrees of murder in the two cases. For example, they could find White guilty of manslaughter in the killing of one victim and of first-degree murder in the other.

Judge Calcagno instructed the jury members that they might use the defendant's character and background to help them determine whether or not he was capable of acting with the *malice*, or deliberate and premeditated intent to kill, required for a first-degree murder conviction. The judge also said that if the jury found that White had acted out of the heat of passion, they must then conclude that he had not necessarily planned the shootings.

YOU ARE THE JUROR.
WHAT IS YOUR DECISION?

This case has caused a sharp and potentially explosive split between San Francisco's conservative and gay communities. You must focus on the case and make your own decision. What verdict do you declare in the charges of murder against Dan White?

Option 1　　**White is guilty of two counts of manslaughter.**

Option 2　　**White is guilty of one count of manslaughter and one count of first-degree murder.**

Option 3　　**White is guilty of two counts of second-degree murder.**

Option 4　　**White is guilty of one count of manslaughter and one count of second-degree murder.**

Option 5　　**White is guilty of two counts of first-degree murder.**

The Dan White defense fund raised $100,000 in contributions, much of it from police and firefighters who had worked with him.

The jurors chose *Option 1*. They returned a verdict that White was guilty of two counts of manslaughter.

A jury of seven women and five men, who had been sequestered for the length of the trial, debated for six days before announcing their verdict of two counts of manslaughter. The only option that they did not seriously consider was *Option 5*, finding White guilty of two counts of first-degree murder. One juror voted for a first-degree murder conviction on the first ballot, but then quickly abandoned that position. The jury, however, debated at length as to whether to convict Dan White of manslaughter or second-degree murder.

After the trial, the jurors—all of whom said they were heterosexual in pretrial questioning—insisted that the issue of homosexuality had never entered their discussions. One juror later explained that he considered Dan White to be a moral man. For this reason, he believed that something unusual must have triggered White's outburst. Another juror, however, hinted that the jury had gone beyond the facts of the case to consider the implications of the verdict. "We didn't want to give the city a worse name," she commented. "We wanted things to just quiet down and be over with."

Judge Calcagno sentenced White to seven years and eight months in prison—the maximum sentence for voluntary manslaughter.

A somber crowd gathered at city hall after the killings.

ANALYSIS

If the jurors hoped their verdict would end San Francisco's turmoil over the killings, they were sadly mistaken. The city's gay community and many other people believed that the jury had basically excused White from responsibility for murder because his victims were a gay man and his political ally. The fact that defense lawyers had managed to dismiss all gays and lesbians (and even people who had gay friends) from the jury compounded their fear and frustration.

On the night of the killings, 30,000 people had held a peaceful candlelight vigil to honor the victims. Now, after the announcement of the verdict, many people in the gay community reacted with rage. Five thousand people rioted, lighting fires, burning police cars, and throwing rocks and bottles. In the uproar, 120 people were injured. While many San Francisco residents—including most police—agreed with the verdict, others expressed disgust with the jury. "It's obscene," said supervisor Harry Britt. "This is an insane jury." Even Mayor Feinstein, who had offered testimony sympathetic to White, commented, "As far as I'm concerned these were two murders."

Many trial observers blamed the verdict on a weak presentation by the prosecutor. They believed Norman had failed to present evidence that White was a bully who had a history of getting into fights. He frequently threw

When the gay community learned of Dan White's verdict, thousands of people began marching from Castro Street to City Hall, chanting "Out of the bars and into the streets!" The protest escalated into a riot and battle with police by nightfall.

tantrums and even sent youth gangs, including Nazis, to political gatherings of opposing candidates. Norman also neglected to bring to light testimony about Harvey Milk's fear of White. In addition, the prosecutor glossed over the fact that White never showed remorse for his victims but had displayed regret only because his actions had gotten him into trouble. While White's lawyers had harped about their client's good character and family values, the prosecutors had failed to give the members of the jury a sense of Supervisor Milk and Mayor Moscone as human beings. To many people, it seemed clear that Dan White had shot two men in cold blood out of revenge—a motive that disallowed a "heat-of-passion" defense. Yet Norman never brought up revenge as a motive.

The case drew national attention because of the unique "Twinkie" defense—the dubious claim that a defendant who eats too much junk food might not be fully responsible for his actions. (Another oversight made by the prosecution was not mentioning that Dan White had *always* eaten a lot of junk food.) As supervisor, Dan White had often scorned arguments that lessened a perpetrator's responsibility for a crime. He had also been a leading proponent of the death penalty for crimes such as those he committed, while his victims, Harvey Milk and George Moscone, had consistently opposed capital punishment.

Dan White served five years of his seven-year sentence and was released from prison in January 1984. Less than two years after he was freed, he committed suicide on October 21, 1985.

6

THE FORD MOTOR CO.
THE PINTO EXPLOSION
1980

On the afternoon of August 10, 1978, Judy Ulrich was driving her sister Lyn and her cousin Donna Ulrich from Osceola, Indiana, to a church volleyball game in nearby Goshen. Before the three girls reached their destination, however, they turned around and headed back toward Osceola. Suddenly, a Chevrolet van slammed into the rear of their 1973 Ford Pinto.

While the van sustained only minor damage, the Pinto burst into a ball of flame. Trapped inside the car, Donna and Lyn burned to death. Judy managed to escape, but not before suffering terrible burns over most of her body. She died eight hours after the accident.

A month later, an Indiana grand jury indicted the Ford Motor Company on three charges of reckless homicide in connection with the accident. This was a historic case because, for the first time ever in the United States, a manufacturer was being held criminally liable for a defective or dangerous product. The case came to trial in Winamac, Indiana, on January 15, 1980.

THE CASE FOR THE PROSECUTION

Prosecutor Michael Cosentino argued that the Ford Motor Company was responsible for the deaths of the three teens because it had cut corners on safety to save money. In the process, Ford had produced an unsafe car.

The key to the prosecution's case was the claim that a relatively minor collision had erupted into a horrific fireball. Albert Clark, a witness for the prosecution, testified that he saw the collision as he and his wife approached the Pinto in the opposite lane. According to Clark, "the force [of the collision] was not that terrific."

The remains of Judy Ulrich's 1973 Ford Pinto after its gas tank exploded in an accident. Judy, her sister Lyn, and their cousin Donna were killed.

Attorney Michael Cosentino speaks with reporters during the historic trial of the Ford Motor Company for reckless homicide.

Clark and several other witnesses testified that the Ulrich car had been moving when the Chevrolet van struck it from behind. This forward motion would have reduced the impact at which the cars collided.

William Martin, who also witnessed the collision, estimated the van was traveling at 50 miles per hour (mph) and the Pinto at 15. Several other witnesses, including Robert Duggar, the van's driver, also placed the difference in velocity between the two vehicles at 30 to 35 mph.

A teenager who had passed the Pinto and saw the accident in her rear-view mirror thought the impact was even less severe. She put the van's speed at 40 to 45 mph and the Pinto's at 30 to 35 mph and slowing. Neil Graves, an Indiana state trooper, noted that when he arrived on the scene, the Pinto was in second gear, indicating that it had been moving.

Prosecutor Cosentino contrasted the relatively low speed of the collision with the tremendous damage sustained by the Pinto. One witness compared the fiery explosion to "a large napalm bomb." The Chevy van, on the other hand, had barely sustained a dent.

The prosecution then brought in two medical experts, who had performed autopsies on the victims, to support the claim that the collision could not have been severe. Dr. Robert Stein reported that the victims had died as a result of the fire, not from internal injuries caused by the collision. Dr. James Benz testified that a back-seat passenger in a high-speed collision would certainly sustain some kind of spinal injury. Lyn Ulrich, who was in the back seat, had suffered no such injuries.

A radiologist noted that Judy Ulrich was fully conscious immediately after the collision. She would very likely have been knocked unconscious in a high-speed collision. In addition, none of the victims suffered the severe skull fractures common in high-speed collisions.

Cosentino then focused on design defects in the Pinto. Trooper Graves described how the gas tank had split wide open in the accident. He testified that he found gasoline on the inside floor of the car. This showed that the Pinto's tank had ruptured in the collision, spraying burning gasoline into the passenger compartment.

The prosecutor noted that the Pinto's fuel tank was located in a vulnerable spot—behind the rear-wheel axle. He pointed out that most cars built in the United States had 26 inches of crush space between the rear bumper and the gas tank. This space would protect the gas tank from the impact of most moderate-speed collisions. The Pinto, however, had only 6 inches of crush space.

Gas tank

Rear bumper

Judy Ulrich's
gas tank

*The underside of a 1973 Ford Pinto turned
sideways shows the gas tank located only one-half
foot from the rear bumper. The badly mangled
gas tank from Judy Ulrich's car is in front.*

Next, the prosecutor introduced evidence to prove
that Ford had known about these defects but had chosen
to ignore them. Harley Copp, a former assistant chief
research engineer at Ford, testified against his old
employer. According to Copp, the design of the car was
not safe. The former Ford engineer claimed that in an
effort to hold down costs, the auto company had equipped
the Pinto with a gas tank designed to withstand collisions
up to only 20 mph.

The prosecution argued that Ford had rushed the Pinto to market with inadequate testing and with a strict specification that it weigh less than 2,000 pounds and cost less than $2,000. Copp claimed that the company could have greatly reduced the danger of fire resulting from a collision with a design change in the Pinto that would have cost less than $7 per car. Ford, charged the prosecutor, had been unwilling to spend even that small amount of money to ensure the safety of Pinto buyers.

As evidence that Ford had known it had a safety problem with the Pinto, prosecutor Cosentino noted that the company had recalled 1.5 million Pintos in June 1978—two months before the fatal accident—in order to repair faulty fuel tanks. How could a company claim it has a safe fuel tank, he asked, while at the same time issuing a costly recall to fix a safety problem with that tank?

Cosentino further noted that although Ford had known the Pinto was unsafe, the company did not inform all of its customers or make any effort to solve the problem until it was too late. Mattie Ulrich, the mother of two of the dead girls, testified that the first warning she received about the car was a form letter in February 1979—eight months after Ford had decided to repair the faulty fuel tanks and nearly six months after the fatal accident that killed her daughters.

Cosentino argued that for the sake of profit, the Ford Motor Company had deliberately disregarded the safety of its customers. He urged the jurors to "send a message" that would be heard "in boardrooms across this country"—a message that would force corporations to take responsibility for the safety of their products.

The Ulrich family—Mattie (in foreground), Earl (in light-colored suit), and Sharon (in turtleneck)— leaves the courtroom.

THE CASE FOR THE DEFENSE

Defense attorney James Neal told the jurors, "We won't even deny that we could be wrong. But we do deny that we are reckless killers." His first order of business was to contradict the prosecution's claims that the impact in the collision was relatively minor.

Levi Woodard Jr., an orderly at Elkhart General Hospital who had been on duty the day of the accident, took the stand for the defense. He said that he had talked to Judy Ulrich in the hours before her death as she was undergoing treatment at the hospital. Judy told him that the three girls had stopped for gas. They had set the gas cap on top of their car and forgotten to put it back on

Ford hired James Neal, who had been a prosecutor in the 1973-74 Watergate hearings, to defend the company against the unprecedented charge of reckless homicide.

again. As they left the station and drove down the high-way, the cap rolled off the car. Judy turned the car around to retrieve the gas cap and put on her emergency flashers. According to Ulrich, the Pinto was stopped when Robert Duggar's Chevrolet van slammed into it.

Dr. Galen Miller, the emergency-room surgeon who had treated Duggar after the accident, also testified that he had been told by Duggar that the Pinto was not moving when he struck it. Virtually all the witnesses at the scene of the accident agreed that Duggar was traveling at around 50 mph at the time of impact.

To reinforce the point that the impact was tremendous, James Neal brought to the stand engineer John Habberstad, who had conducted crash tests at a Ford facility. Habberstad reported that based on similar test crashes using 1972 Chevrolet vans like the model Duggar drove, he estimated that Duggar had slammed into the Pinto at a minimum speed of 55 mph. No car, he stated, is built to withstand a collision at that rate of speed.

Neal then called Douglas Toms, the former head of the National Highway Traffic Safety Administration (NHTSA), to the stand. Toms testified that the 1973 Pinto was a "very conventional" automobile and was no more likely to burst into flames from a rear-end collision than any other subcompact manufactured that year.

Other automotive experts backed up this testimony with their opinion that the Pinto's design and construction were comparable to other subcompacts. Professional race-car driver Tom Sneva took the stand to say that he actually preferred the gas-tank location in the Pinto. James Schultz, a former engineer with Chrysler, testified that the Pinto was comparable—and in some ways even superior—to its competitors in safety design.

Next, the attorney for Ford brought forth statistics to counter those of the prosecution. In cross-examination, Neal forced prosecution witness Byron Bloch to admit that between the years of 1968 and 1977 about 90 percent of the passenger cars manufactured in the United States had fuel tanks located behind the rear axle.

The defense dismissed the suggestion that Ford had callously built and sold a car that the company knew to be unsafe. Neal called to the witness stand Harold MacDonald, a Ford executive who had helped to design the Pinto. MacDonald stated that he knew better than anyone the need for a safe fuel system because his own father had died in a car accident when his gas tank erupted into flames. Not only did MacDonald drive a Pinto, but he also had bought one for his own son. The defense asked the jury to consider whether anyone would put his own life and the life of his child at risk by driving a car that was even suspected to be unsafe.

Neal noted that even though Ford believed the Pinto to be safe, it had listened to its customers and to reports of problems. The defense then called on experts to testify that Ford had cooperated with NHTSA to produce a recall kit that would make the Pinto even safer. Ford had worked around the clock to produce the kit and to alert its customers as quickly as possible.

Instead of blaming Ford for the problem, Neal suggested that people place the blame where it belonged—on Robert Duggar. Neal noted that Duggar was a careless driver with a record of committing driving violations. Had he been paying attention to the road and not reaching down to pick something off the floor of his Chevy at the crucial moment, the Ulrich girls would be alive. "No car can ever be fully safe from reckless drivers on the road," argued Neal. The defense attorney insisted that Duggar, not Ford, had caused the deaths.

The defense also placed blame on the faulty design of the road on which the collision had taken place. The road had no shoulder at the point where the accident occurred, and the concrete curb was so high that the Ulrichs had not been able to pull off the road when they stopped to retrieve the Pinto's gas cap. Instead, they were in a vulnerable position—stuck in the middle of a high-speed road. The defense attorney argued that had the road been designed properly, the accident would never have occurred. Highway 33, Neal insisted, had much more to do with the deaths than the Pinto's design.

The defense concluded with testimony showing that the 1973 Pinto had met or exceeded every fuel-system safety standard required by the U.S. government at the

A publicity photo of the 1973 Ford Pinto. The economical Pinto was a popular choice for first-time car buyers.

time it was produced. Ford was obeying the laws. How could a company that followed all the laws and regulations be guilty of criminal conduct? How could any business operate if every state court began imposing its own standards of safety and prosecuting companies on criminal charges for violations of regulations that didn't even exist when their products had been manufactured?

THE PROSECUTION'S REBUTTAL

Prosecutor Cosentino pointed out to the jury that most of the witnesses called by the defense to testify about the safety of the Pinto were Ford employees with huge salaries. The prosecutor noted that these witnesses had a strong incentive to give testimony that would help Ford to win its case. Even former NHTSA head Douglas Toms was not an unbiased government observer. Retired from government service, Toms was the owner of a recreational-vehicle company that did $1 million in business with Ford in 1979.

Finally, another lawyer on the prosecution team urged jurors to weigh whose conduct was more criminal: Robert Duggar's momentary lapse of concentration or the Ford Motor Company's six years of neglect of the Pinto's safety problems.

LEGAL ISSUES

The case brought against Ford was unique in the history of the American legal system. Never before had any law-enforcement agency brought criminal charges against a corporation because of an injury caused by a product. Only relatively recently had the courts allowed the public any kind of recourse in dealings with corporations. Prior to 1916, the courts did not even permit an individual to file a civil suit against a corporation for injury due to a defective product.

The Pinto case was mainly symbolic. Even if the jury found Ford guilty on three counts, the maximum penalty would be a $30,000 fine. For the nation's third-largest corporation—a company whose 1979 sales totaled $42 billion—such a fine would be mere pocket change.

Of far greater concern to Ford was the potential loss of sales because of negative publicity, particularly if the jury should find the company guilty of producing dangerous cars.

In determining who was at fault for the deaths, Judge Harold Staffeldt offered the following instruction: If the jurors believed that Ford, the defendant, had contributed to the deaths of the three girls, then they had to consider Ford responsible, even if others had also played a role in the accident. In other words, even if Robert Duggar and the faulty road design were major factors in the deaths, Ford was also responsible if its actions had contributed to the severity of the accident. The jury was to be the sole judge of whether or not Ford had operated within the boundaries of acceptable conduct.

YOU ARE THE JUROR.
WHAT IS YOUR DECISION?

What verdict do you declare in the charges that Ford is criminally at fault in the deaths of the three teenagers?

Option 1   **The Ford Motor Company is guilty.**

Option 2   **The Ford Motor Company is not guilty.**

On the day the Pinto verdict was announced, the board of directors met at Ford's corporate headquarters in Dearborn, Michigan, and Henry Ford II stepped down as chairman. For the first time, the company was run by someone outside the Ford family.

The jurors chose *Option 2*. They found Ford not guilty on all three counts of reckless homicide.

After hearing eight weeks of testimony, a jury of seven men and five women initially split 8 to 4, with the majority voting to acquit Ford. Two of the four who had at first favored the conviction of Ford changed their minds after many hours of deliberation. But the remaining two held firm. With the vote stuck at 10 to 2, the judge asked the jury members if they felt they could reach a decision. They said no. Noting the time and expense of the trial, Judge Staffeldt asked them to deliberate a while longer.

Finally, after 25 hours of discussion and 25 ballots, the jury voted to acquit Ford. Most of the jurors agreed that the Pinto was about as safe as other subcompacts and that the high speed of the impact had caused the explosion.

But that vote did not mean the jury had accepted Ford's version of the case. Most jurors were persuaded by the prosecution's story that the Pinto was moving, and most believed the Pinto was not a safe car. Their verdict simply meant they were not convinced that Ford had acted recklessly in producing the Pinto or in failing to warn customers about the car once the company knew there were problems.

James Yurgilas, the last juror to switch his vote to acquittal, reluctantly went along with the majority. "I felt that [the Pinto] was a reckless automobile," he later said. "But on the other hand, you couldn't prove that they didn't do everything in their power to recall it. They got off only through a loophole."

Six of the jurors at a press conference following the acquittal on March 13, 1980: (front, left to right) Arthur Selmer (the jury foreman), Raymond Schramm, Barbara Asel; (back, left to right) Charlotte Berger, James Yurgilas, Jay Chamness.

ANALYSIS

The judge's refusal to allow the prosecution to introduce much of its evidence into the court records had exasperated Michael Cosentino. The prosecutor had results of test crashes and dozens of other documents (including photographs, reports, and memos) that showed Ford had been aware of a safety problem with the Pinto model as early as 1970—three years before the car that exploded had even been produced.

Virtually all the damaging evidence about the Pinto's unsafe design, however, had come from Pintos manufactured before or after the 1973 model. This information did not help the prosecution because Judge Harold

Staffeldt decided that he would allow Cosentino to introduce only evidence pertaining to the 1973-model Pinto involved in the crash. Some jurors later expressed resentment that the judge had barred evidence that might have helped them decide the case differently.

The "not guilty" verdict was a major victory for Ford, which had the financial resources to outspend the prosecution by hundreds of thousands of dollars. A guilty verdict would have hurt Ford badly in civil suits filed against the company in connection with other Pinto accidents. Unlike the case concerning the deaths of the three teenagers, a civil suit would not charge Ford with criminal acts. Instead, the civil suit would ask the auto company to

Members of the media prepare for the press conference after the jury acquitted Ford.

reimburse the claimants for damages they had suffered while using the company's product. Being found guilty of criminal charges would have provided powerful evidence for filing expensive civil suits claiming that Ford had manufactured a product that was unsafe.

Nonetheless, the Ford Motor Company did not emerge unscathed from the trial. Its legal victory could not erase weeks of bad publicity. Even several of the jurors who had voted to acquit Ford of criminal charges had strong doubts about the Pinto's safety. Consumer concern generated by the trial may have contributed to Ford's loss of more than $1 billion in its U.S. operations in 1981.

Legal analysts also note that although the prosecution did not win a conviction, it broke new legal ground. Prior to this case, no U.S. manufacturer had ever been charged with and stood trial for a criminal act involving the marketing of an unsafe product. The fact that prosecutor Cosentino was able to bring the case before a jury paved the way for similar legal actions against other companies. Future jury decisions could play a role in shaping American manufacturing either by forcing companies to produce safer products or by driving up the cost of products when consumers file frivolous lawsuits in the hope of extorting millions of dollars from manufacturers.

7

BERNHARD GOETZ
"THE SUBWAY VIGILANTE"
1987

Shortly after noon on December 22, 1984, a white man entered a New York City subway car. Four black youths—Troy Canty, Darrell Cabey, Barry Allen, and James Ramseur—approached him and asked for money. The man whipped out a gun and shot each of the teenagers. None of the shots was fatal, but Darrell Cabey was paralyzed.

After a highly publicized search for the "Subway Vigilante," Bernhard Goetz surrendered to police in Concord, New Hampshire, on December 31. Convinced that he was about to be "beaten into a pulp," Goetz maintained in his confession that he had acted in self-defense.

Nonetheless, New York City prosecutors charged Goetz with 13 crimes, ranging in seriousness from carrying a loaded gun without a permit to assault and attempted murder against each of the four youths.

Prosecutor Gregory Waples had to overcome the presumption of the majority of New Yorkers that the defendant was a righteous crimefighter.

THE CASE FOR THE PROSECUTION

Prosecutor Gregory Waples relied heavily on Goetz's taped confession to argue his case. In the confession, Goetz freely admitted that, in violation of the law, he had carried a loaded gun for which he had no permit.

Goetz's description of the events on the subway clearly pointed to his guilt on both the assault and the attempted murder charges. He described how he found himself at one end of the subway compartment next to the four youths. "How are you?" they asked Goetz.

"Fine," he replied.

Then at least two of the youths came toward Goetz and stood between him and the riders at the other end of the compartment. The others also stood close by.

"Give me five dollars," Troy Canty said.

At that point, Goetz said he saw one of Canty's buddies put a hand into a bulging coat pocket.

"What did you say?" Goetz asked.

When Canty repeated that he wanted money, Bernhard Goetz stood up, drew his gun, and quickly shot each of the four teenagers in succession. Although he claimed that he had acted in self-defense, in some of his statements to the police, Goetz admitted that his intention had been "to murder them, to hurt them, to make them suffer as much as possible."

According to the prosecutor, Goetz had not simply been defending himself. Rather, he had deliberately paralyzed the young man in cold blood. In his confession, the defendant described seeing Darrell Cabey sitting in a subway seat after he had been shot. In Goetz's own words, he then approached Cabey and said, "You seem to be all right; here's another." With that, Goetz shot Cabey a second time.

A half-dozen witnesses who saw the subway shooting backed up Goetz's story in most respects. All agreed that the four teenage boys did not physically attack Goetz and that Goetz shot all four. One witness, Christopher Boucher, was standing only 40 feet away during the incident. His description of the shooting of Darrell Cabey was almost identical to Goetz's. Boucher said that the defendant had approached to within two or three feet of the young man. Then he looked down at him and shot him.

The state argued that even if the four youths had posed a threat to Goetz, the danger was not serious enough to warrant Goetz's actions. None of the four had possessed a gun or knife. The three screwdrivers they carried, argued the prosecutor, were not weapons but burglary tools.

Bernhard Goetz is surrounded by photographers as he arrives at court. The case was front-page news in every New York newspaper for the duration of the trial.

Furthermore, the prosecutor noted, even if Goetz had believed the four young men were a danger to him, he had no justification for his last shot at a helpless, wounded Cabey, who clearly was in no condition to pose any further threat. According to Waples, Bernhard Goetz's actions made a "mockery of the notion of self-defense." The prosecutor insisted that what the defendant had done in the name of self-defense was "ugly," "cold-blooded," and "savage."

The state maintained that Goetz had taken the law into his own hands. Waples asked the jurors to imagine what the United States would be like if everyone decided to ignore the law and punish those whom they felt had wronged them.

THE CASE FOR THE DEFENSE

Defense attorney Barry Slotnick maintained that each of the four youths was a dangerous person with a criminal record. Just two months before the subway incident, the police had arrested Darrell Cabey for armed robbery, and Troy Canty and James Ramseur had served time in prison for theft. The courts had earlier convicted Barry Allen of two counts of disorderly conduct, one of which involved threatening a woman.

According to the defense, the four were not helpless kids but "predators of society." The defense noted that in his brief appearance on the witness stand, James Ramseur had demonstrated exactly what type of people Goetz had encountered. Sullen, insolent, and hostile, Ramseur refused to answer even routine questions. Witnesses to the shooting reported that the youths were rowdy and loud and had used filthy language while riding the subway.

Defense attorney Slotnick also pointed out that the four young men had approached Goetz in a threatening manner, cutting him off from the rest of the people in the subway car and demanding money. They did not even try to hide the fact that they intended to rob Goetz.

Police detective Peter Smith appeared as a defense witness. Shortly after Goetz shot Canty, the detective spoke to the wounded youth. According to Smith, Canty said, "We were going to rob him but the white guy shot us first." Detective Charles Penelton testified that while Canty was being treated for his wounds in the hospital, he admitted that "we surrounded the white guy."

The defense attorney argued that Goetz had a particularly strong reason to fear the youths who surrounded him. In 1981, he had been mugged on the streets of New York City. That attack had left him with a permanently damaged knee and had scarred him emotionally. To protect himself from future attacks, Goetz had applied for a permit to carry a gun. When city officials denied his request, Goetz felt that he had no choice but to carry a gun illegally.

The defense for Goetz noted that when the youths approached him, he had only a moment to assess the situation. When he looked into their eyes, he saw a threat. As he told investigators in his confession, he was afraid of being "beaten into a pulp." Trapped on a subway car by four threatening youths asking for money, Goetz had merely reacted in self-defense.

Bernhard Goetz (center) speaks with his attorneys, Mark Baker (left) and Barry Slotnick outside the courthouse. During the trial, Slotnick contended that Goetz's victims were dangerous criminals who had posed a real threat to his client.

According to defense attorney Barry Slotnick, the jury could not expect Goetz to assess his every action calmly and carefully once he started to defend himself. Psychologist Bernard Yudwitz testified that in situations such as this the rational mind shuts down. Instead, a threatened person defending himself or herself will act on "automatic pilot" without conscious thought.

Furthermore, the defense asserted that Goetz's story about going up to the wounded Cabey and shooting him again out of sheer malice was not true. At the time of the confession, Goetz was in a confused state of mind and was not able to report all the facts accurately. While his taped confession to police sounded as though he had deliberately walked up to a wounded victim and shot him again, the event actually happened much more quickly than that.

In fact, only one witness to the subway incident, Christopher Boucher, testified that time had elapsed between the next-to-last and final shots. Eight other eyewitnesses agreed that Goetz had fired his shots in rapid succession. The defense attorney argued that if there had been no interruption between shots, then all the shots fired by Goetz were part of his defensive reaction to the four menacing youths.

Medical evidence provided by the defense's expert witness refuted the allegation that Goetz had shot the wounded, sitting Cabey. According to New York City medical examiner Dominick Dimaio, the angle of the entry of the bullet was such that Cabey could not have been sitting when Goetz shot him.

Slotnick argued that the four victims in this case got "what the law allowed." Bernhard Goetz had acted as any rational person would to defend himself. The victims, stated Slotnick, had no one to blame for their injuries but themselves.

THE PROSECUTOR'S REBUTTAL

Prosecutor Waples noted that no one on the defense team had disputed Goetz's account of the shooting except for his walking over to shoot Cabey a second time. How could Goetz be so accurate in recounting the rest of the incident, he asked the jury, but so wrong about the second shot he fired at Cabey?

Waples brought in Dr. Charles Hirsch, the Suffolk County medical examiner, to contradict the defense's expert witness who had claimed the angle of the shot meant that Cabey could not have been sitting. Hirsch testified that his review of the evidence indicated Cabey could indeed have been sitting.

In his rebuttal, Waples made no attempt to portray the four youths as innocent young men. But he quoted a decision handed down by the New York Supreme Court nearly a century before. That court had said that "the law protects everyone from unlawful violence, regardless of his character." Thus, Waples insisted, even if Canty, Cabey, Ramseur, and Allen had been looking for trouble, the law still protected them from an attack as vicious as Goetz's had been.

LEGAL ISSUES

The prosecution had charged Goetz with carrying a loaded gun in public without a permit, assault, and attempted murder. Judge Stephen Crane reminded the jurors that the U.S. system of justice always presumes that a defendant is innocent until proven guilty. For this reason, the judge explained, "where two inferences may be reasonably drawn, one consistent with innocence and the other consistent with guilt, the defendant is entitled to the inference of innocence." In other words, if the jury hears a reasonable interpretation of the facts that indicates the defendant is innocent and another reasonable interpretation that indicates the defendant is guilty, the jury must assume the defendant to be innocent. But if the jurors find beyond a reasonable doubt that Goetz committed these crimes and that he did not act in self-defense, then they must convict Goetz.

YOU ARE THE JUROR.
WHAT IS YOUR DECISION?

No one disputes the fact that Goetz had carried a loaded gun without a permit and shot all four teenagers. You must decide whether his actions were an entirely justifiable act of self-defense or were instead beyond the bounds of self-defense. What verdict do you declare?

Option 1   **Goetz is guilty of carrying a loaded gun without a permit, assault with a deadly weapon, and attempted murder.**

Option 2   **Goetz is guilty of carrying a loaded gun without a permit and assault with a deadly weapon, but he is not guilty of attempted murder.**

Option 3   **Goetz is guilty of carrying a loaded gun without a permit, but he is not guilty of the other two charges.**

Option 4   **Goetz is not guilty of all three charges.**

In the two and one-half years since his arrest in December 1984, Bernhard Goetz had nearly lost his electronics business because of unrelenting publicity.

The jurors chose *Option 3*. They found Goetz guilty of carrying a loaded gun without a permit but not guilty of the other two charges.

The mostly white jury took only 30 minutes to convict Goetz of criminal possession of a weapon. His belief that he needed a weapon and his inability to get a permit did not change the fact that he had violated the law.

In deciding the other two charges, the jurors faced a tougher task. Their initial poll showed four jurors leaning toward not guilty on the charges of attempted murder and eight undecided. The jurors threw out the charges of attempted murder because they decided that in order to attempt murder, a person needed a motive for murdering. When Goetz fired the shots, the jury decided, he did so not with the primary intention of murdering anyone but simply to protect himself from attack.

The most hotly debated charge in the jury room was that of assault. On this, the members fell back on the "reasonable doubt" requirement. Because of conflicting testimony, they could not be certain that Goetz had not acted in self-defense during the entire incident.

Due to the serious injuries that resulted from Goetz's actions and because he showed no inclination to obey the gun law in the future, Judge Crane imposed a harsh sentence for the charge of criminal gun possession. He sentenced Goetz to six months in jail, four and one-half years of probation, 280 hours of community service, psychiatric counseling, and a fine of $5,075.

After the jury delivered the verdict in the Goetz case on June 16, 1987, the Guardian Angels, a group that advocates self-defense against criminals, escorted Goetz from the courthouse as reporters swarmed in.

ANALYSIS

In trials, emotions sometimes outweigh facts. Jurors had a particularly hard time setting aside their feelings in this case. Despite the permanently crippling injuries that Cabey had suffered, the questionable character of the victims reduced the chances that the jury could sympathize with them. Judge Crane commented that Ramseur's belligerent appearance on the witness stand had conveyed a "viciousness and selfishness more eloquently than words could."

Furthermore, many Americans were fed up with the increasing level of crime on the streets and the apparent inability of law enforcement to provide safety. According to a March 1985 Gallup poll, 57 percent of Americans supported Goetz. Many, in fact, applauded his actions because they believed that if more citizens stood up against criminals, the United States would be a far safer place. Curtis Sliwa, leader of the Guardian Angels, said the acquittal of Goetz on the assault and attempted murder charges "sent a message to all decent people that it's OK to fight back."

Other people, however, believed the decision was racist. Some Americans feared that the verdict represented the belief that shooting blacks was acceptable behavior, even if such actions technically violated the law.

The Goetz case raised many questions about the role of self-defense and the right to own firearms, as well as the role of law enforcement and racial fears and stereotypes. As often happens, the jury's verdict decided only a particular case and did nothing to settle any of these deeper social issues that were a part of the trial.

In the years since the shootings, people continue to debate whether Bernhard Goetz was defending himself or unleashing pent-up rage.

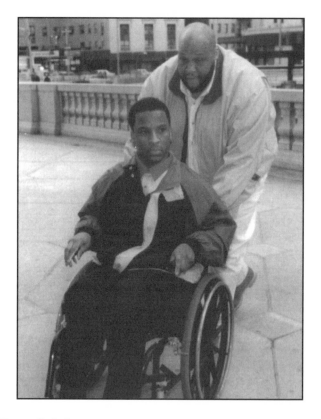

Darrell Cabey arrives in court in April 1996. Brain damage he suffered as a result of the shooting has left him with diminished mental capacity.

Nine years after the criminal trial against Bernhard Goetz, the family of Darrell Cabey, the youth who had been paralyzed in the shooting, won a civil suit against the gunman. In April 1996, a jury awarded Cabey $43 million in damages for the injuries he had suffered in the incident. The other youths—who never sued Goetz—have all been arrested on various charges in the years following the shooting, and James Ramseur was convicted for a rape he committed just six months after he was shot.

8

O. J. SIMPSON
JUSTICE FOR "THE JUICE"?
1995

L ate on the night of June 12, 1994, residents of an affluent neighborhood in Los Angeles discovered the bloody bodies of Nicole Brown Simpson and Ronald Goldman lying near a gate outside Simpson's luxury townhouse. The stabbings made front-page news because Nicole was the glamorous ex-wife of football superstar and Hollywood actor O. J. Simpson.

In the early morning hours of June 13, police went to Simpson's residence to inform him of the deaths. Simpson was in Chicago, but evidence found at the murder scene and at his house made him the prime suspect.

The media glare grew white-hot as police charged one of America's most popular celebrities with two gruesome murders. After more than seven months of haggling over evidence and preparing for the case, opening arguments in the trial began on January 24, 1995.

O. J. and Nicole Brown Simpson in happier days

THE CASE FOR THE PROSECUTION

Marcia Clark and Christopher Darden presented the bulk of the prosecution's case. They first established that, despite his public image as a likable sports star, Simpson was capable of violent behavior. Detective John Edwards described a police visit to the Simpsons' home that took place in the early morning hours of New Year's Day in 1989. Edwards reported that he had found Nicole hiding in the bushes outside the house, partially clothed. Her face was bruised, and she was terrified. "He's going to kill me," she told the officer, referring to Simpson. For that incident, a California court sentenced Simpson to two years probation and a $700 fine.

Prosecutors then played for the jury a tape recording of an emergency 911 call Nicole had made in October 1993. On the tape, Nicole frantically begged for protection from Simpson after he broke down the door of her house. "He's going nuts! He's out of control!" she cried.

In the background of the recording, jurors could hear Simpson shouting profanities. Denise Brown, Nicole's sister, described other incidents in which Simpson had physically and verbally abused his wife. While at their daughter's recital on the day of the murders, Brown said, Simpson kept staring at Nicole with a frightening look, his eyes "glazed over."

Prosecutor Clark next brought in witnesses to establish a timeline for the murders. A neighbor of Nicole's, Pablo Fenjves, testified that he had heard a dog's "plaintive wail" between 10:15 and 10:20 P.M. Steven Schwab, another neighbor, reported that he had found Nicole's dog wandering shortly after 10:40 P.M. Obviously, said Clark, the wail noted by Fenjves was made by the dog in reaction to the murder of Nicole.

Christopher Darden, a prosecutor experienced with murder cases, repeatedly clashed with defense attorneys over what evidence should be admitted into the trial.

The time of the murders was important because Simpson had no reliable alibi for where he was at that time. Simpson's houseguest, Brian "Kato" Kaelin, had last seen him at about 9:35 P.M. No one saw Simpson again until nearly 11 o'clock that same night.

Simpson's whereabouts became even more curious because of the testimony of limousine driver Allan Park, who had driven to Simpson's home the night of the murders to take the celebrity to the airport for a late flight to Chicago. Park was a valuable witness for the prosecution because he had kept to a strict time schedule.

Although Park was not due to pick up Simpson until 10:45 P.M., the driver arrived early to make sure he could find the residence. He drove by Simpson's driveway at 10:22 and then drove around the corner to the front gate. He waited awhile, then buzzed the intercom by the locked gate. No one answered.

As time passed, Park buzzed several more times, but there was no answer. At that point, he called his employer and asked what to do. His boss told him to keep waiting. At 10:55 P.M., Park saw a large African American man of about Simpson's size dash into the house from the yard. A few minutes later, Simpson finally answered the intercom. Apologizing for his tardiness, he explained that he had overslept and had not heard the intercom because he was in the shower. Park later testified that when Simpson finally showed up with his travel bags, he appeared a bit rushed and frantic.

When officers arrived at Simpson's house in the early hours of the morning, they found his white Ford Bronco by the curb. Park, the limousine driver, testified that the Bronco had not been there when he arrived at the residence.

In a statement to police, Simpson had claimed that Park had seen him enter the house because he had been on his lawn chipping golf balls. The prosecution pointed out that this story contradicted what Simpson himself had told Park on the intercom and argued that the lack of an explanation for O. J. Simpson's whereabouts at the time of the murders was strong evidence of his guilt.

The testimony of Kato Kaelin was even more damaging. Kaelin told the court that shortly before 11 o'clock he had heard three thumps on the wall of his room in the guest house. Next to the wall—on the narrow path that Simpson would have had to take to get from his Bronco on the street into his house without running into Park at the front gate—was an air conditioner. Prosecutors

Prosecutors Marcia Clark and Christopher Darden question Kato Kaelin about O. J. Simpson's activities the night of the murders. A map of Simpson's estate is on the witness stand beside Kaelin.

claimed that Simpson must have caused the noise by bumping into the air conditioner.

The prosecution then presented more evidence linking Simpson to the murders. Detective Tom Lange told the court that a set of bloody shoe prints leading away from the murder scene were a size 12—Simpson's shoe size. Shoe experts said the prints came from a pair of Bruno Magli shoes, an expensive brand that only someone as wealthy as Simpson was likely to own.

Police also found drops of blood on the left side of the shoe prints. Since those drops did not fade away, they must have dripped from a fresh wound the assailant had suffered. Detective Phil Vannater testified that when he talked to Simpson the day after the murders, the actor had two cuts on the fingers of his left hand. The prosecution then produced photographs of the cuts.

This was only the beginning of the trail of blood that tied Simpson to the crime. Police testified that after discovering tiny smears of blood on the door and the frame of the Ford Bronco, they scaled the wall of Simpson's estate at 4:30 A.M. on the night of the murders. Detective Vannater reported that police investigators found drops of blood leading from the driveway into Simpson's house, a drop of blood on the hardwood floor inside the house, and more blood on a pair of socks at the foot of Simpson's bed.

Police detective Mark Fuhrman found a large, bloody, black leather glove on the path near the spot where Kaelin had heard the thumps. This glove matched one that Robert Riske, the first police officer on the murder scene, had found near the bodies of Nicole Brown Simpson and Ron Goldman. Blood samples at the murder scene matched Simpson's blood type and pointed to him as the killer.

Moreover, Robin Cotton, director of Cellmark Diagnostics, the DNA-testing laboratory that the Los Angeles Police Department had used, explained the results of a sophisticated DNA-fingerprinting process. All people have genetic markers in their chemical makeup that experts can use to distinguish one person's DNA (deoxyribonucleic acid) from someone else's. This testing technique, Cotton explained, is now considered to be scientifically reliable. Cotton's laboratory determined that DNA in blood found at the crime scene matched the DNA patterns of Simpson's blood, and DNA in the blood on the sock by Simpson's bed matched Nicole's blood. Goldman's DNA was in the blood on the leather glove found at Simpson's estate and also in the blood in

Simpson's Bronco. The odds against the DNA belonging to three other people were astronomical—less than one in several hundred million.

Investigators found that the fiber and hair evidence also pointed to Simpson's guilt. FBI fiber experts found hair matching Simpson's on Ron Goldman's shirt. Other FBI analysts testified that a distinctive fiber from a knit ski cap at the murder scene was discovered in Simpson's Ford Bronco, on the bloody gloves, and in the socks found by Simpson's bed.

Then there was the matter of the mysterious bag. Kato Kaelin testified that a knapsack was sitting on the driveway just before Simpson and the limousine left for the airport. Kaelin offered to help Simpson load the bag in the limo, but Simpson had insisted on loading it himself. Allan Park testified that Simpson placed five bags in the car before they left the house. Later, however, witnesses at the airport said Simpson had only four bags. The prosecutors noted that this mysterious missing bag could easily explain why investigators had never found any bloody clothes—Simpson could have disposed of them in the bag, perhaps in an airport trash can.

Prosecutors Clark and Darden maintained that all this evidence pointed to an obsessive, jealous, violent O. J. Simpson killing his ex-wife out of anger because she no longer wanted to be with him. The two lawyers argued that Simpson had killed Goldman simply because he was caught in the wrong place at the wrong time. (Goldman, a waiter at the Mezzaluna restaurant, had gone to Nicole's house to return a pair of sunglasses that someone in her family had left behind after eating at the restaurant.)

Simpson could not account for his whereabouts from 9:36 to 10:55 P.M. According to the prosecution, that was enough time for him to commit the murders and make the 10-minute drive back to his house. The victims of this crime "are telling you who did it with their hair, their clothes, their bodies, their blood," Marcia Clark told the jurors. "Will you hear them?"

The crime scene showed that Ronald Goldman, an aspiring actor, had fought violently for his life. The glasses he was returning to Nicole Brown Simpson were found next to his body. Shortly before she was murdered, Nicole had put her children to bed and had spoken with her mother on the telephone.

THE CASE FOR THE DEFENSE

Because of their past successes, the defense team—led by high-priced attorneys Johnnie Cochran, Robert Shapiro, Barry Scheck, and F. Lee Bailey—was often referred to by the media as "the dream team." They argued that the police had rushed to the conclusion that Simpson was guilty. To convict him, they had tampered with the evidence and then had lied to cover up their deceit.

The defense concentrated their attack on Mark Fuhrman, the detective who had found the second glove at Simpson's estate. They noted that Fuhrman had gone alone down the dark path at Simpson's home, even though other officers at the scene could have accompanied him. He claimed to have found the glove on this path, but no one had seen him find it. Attorney F. Lee Bailey noted that Fuhrman had the opportunity to take one of the gloves left at the murder scene and plant it on Simpson's property.

Attorneys for the defense argued that Fuhrman's motive was that he was a racist who wanted to frame a black man. On the witness stand, Fuhrman swore that during the preceding 10 years, he had never referred to an African American as a "nigger." But witness Kathleen Bell testified that Fuhrman had told her he wished whites could gather and burn all "niggers."

In testifying for the defense, screenwriter Laura Hart McKinney said that she had recorded a number of taped interviews with Fuhrman between 1985 and 1994. On those tapes, Fuhrman had used the word "nigger" 41 times. Jurors heard proof of this in two excerpts from the tapes. This demonstrated not only that Fuhrman was a "genocidal racist," as Cochran had described him, but also that he was a liar.

The prosecutors were unsuccessful in their attempt to keep evidence of Mark Fuhrman's racial hatred out of the trial.

The defense also argued that Fuhrman was not the only liar among the police witnesses. Convicted mobster Craig Fiato said he knew for a fact that Detective Vannater lied when he said the police did not immediately suspect Simpson as the murderer.

In a police videotape of Simpson's bedroom shown by the defense, no socks were evident. Frederic Rieders, the defense's toxicologist, testified that he had found traces of EDTA, a preservative, in the blood on the sock that the prosecution had introduced into evidence. According to this expert witness, the EDTA indicated that the police could have taken the blood from another source and planted it on the sock. According to defense lawyer Barry Scheck, the police had "played with this sock" and had sprinkled blood at the crime scene.

The defense then brought up further evidence that pointed toward a police frame-up. Allan Park, the limousine driver, said he had seen no blood at the estate. And the man who had towed Simpson's Bronco away to be impounded as evidence did not see any blood on the vehicle. Furthermore, the glove that Fuhrman supposedly found on Simpson's property was still moist hours after the murder. If the glove had laid on the ground for hours, as the prosecution contended, why hadn't the blood dried? And why had there been no blood on the ground where Fuhrman found the glove?

Dr. Michael Baden testified that the crime scene showed evidence of a terrific struggle between the murderer or murderers and the victims. If Simpson was involved in such a bloody killing, why was there so little

Barry Scheck, a lawyer with expertise in challenging DNA evidence, argued in court that the Los Angeles Police Department was a "black hole," where evidence disappeared or became tainted without explanation.

Johnnie Cochran was already one of the best-known and most respected trial lawyers in Los Angeles when he joined the Simpson defense team. He quickly took the leading role on the team and formed the defense strategy of challenging the credibility of the police department.

blood on him, and why didn't the police discover any blood stains on the white carpet in his house? And if Simpson had arrived home only minutes before he answered the intercom, how could he have had time to clean up all the blood before leaving for the airport?

Cochran showed the jury a videotape of a crime scene virtually crawling with police and argued that the officers had contaminated the scene. For example, expert crime investigator Henry Lee claimed the police missed footprints that could have belonged to a second murderer. And detectives had thrown one of Nicole's blankets over her body. The hairs and fibers found in the blanket could have come from a previous visit by Simpson to Nicole's house.

The defense also noted that, before depositing it as evidence, Detective Vannater had carried with him the blood collected at the murder scene and then had stored the blood in a plastic envelope at room temperature, which could have caused deterioration of the sample. In addition, Simpson's attorneys pointed out that the police could not account for all of the blood sample they had taken from Simpson. What happened to the missing blood? Defense lawyers claimed police had the means to plant that blood as evidence to implicate O. J. Simpson.

Furthermore, defense witnesses cast doubt on some of the DNA evidence. DNA expert John Gerdes testified that present DNA-testing procedures still had too many inconsistencies and problems to be considered absolutely reliable.

Defense lawyers next introduced evidence that challenged the prosecution's timeline for the murders. Six witnesses who lived in Nicole's neighborhood said they heard no barking dogs before 10:30 P.M. But, Simpson's attorneys argued, if Simpson had committed the murders after 10:30, he would have had little time to get home and dispose of the evidence before leaving for the airport.

In addition, defense lawyers sought to create doubt on a wide range of prosecution testimony. Simpson's personal physician testified that Simpson suffered so badly from arthritis and football injuries that he was not capable of committing the murders. "I wouldn't hire him to back me up in a bar fight," the doctor said. They also suggested that the murders might have been drug-related because one of Nicole's friends was a drug abuser.

Witnesses who saw Simpson at his daughter's recital the afternoon of the murders reported that he was in good spirits at the time, and a videotape taken at the recital backed up their testimony. Airline passengers who had seen Simpson on the flight to Chicago immediately after the murders said that he had been friendly and relaxed and had not acted unusual in any way.

Ironically, part of the prosecution's presentation became central to the defense case. Christopher Darden asked Simpson to try on the glove that police had found at the murder scene. While wearing latex gloves to protect the evidence, Simpson struggled to get the glove on his hand. Grimacing, he complained it didn't fit.

In his closing statement, Johnnie Cochran urged the jury to send a message that police corruption and racism would no longer be tolerated. He insisted that if the jurors did not do what was "right," then this corruption and racism would "continue on forever."

The prosecution spent much of the rest of the trial trying to minimize the damage caused by Christopher Darden's decision to ask Simpson to try on the glove.

THE PROSECUTION'S REBUTTAL

The prosecution admitted that police investigators had made some errors in collecting and processing evidence, but they insisted these mistakes were the kind of honest errors that occur when any police staff is overworked and underfunded. The prosecutors maintained that none of these blunders had affected the evidence that pointed toward Simpson's guilt.

As for Mark Fuhrman, the prosecution admitted he was a despicable character. "Do we wish there were no such person on the planet? Yes," said Marcia Clark. But blood was found in so many places and in such microscopic amounts that Fuhrman simply could not possibly have planted all of it. Furthermore, if the police were as incompetent as the defense claimed them to be, how could they have masterminded the most widespread and intricate framing and cover-up in police history?

Regarding the claim that the gloves did not fit, prosecutors contended that Simpson was exaggerating the tightness. The gloves had shrunk after being soaked with blood, and the latex gloves Simpson was wearing while trying on the gloves had made it difficult to slide them on. Another pair of gloves that were the same size and model as those placed in evidence fit easily when Simpson tried them on without the latex protection. In addition, an official at Aris Isotoner, the manufacturer of the glove found at the crime scene, testified that in photographs the prosecution presented as evidence, Simpson was wearing that model of glove—and the company had made only a few hundred pairs of them.

Police experts testified that the murders had been swift and brutal. Trapped against a fence in a small area, Ron Goldman had no room to maneuver. Because he was too busy trying to ward off lethal blows, he was not able to inflict any injury beyond the two small cuts on Simpson's hand.

The prosecution also produced expert witnesses to contradict what Christopher Darden called the defense's "smoke and mirrors." FBI lab expert Roger Martz testified that the blood sample from the socks contained no EDTA preservative and thus did not point to any tampering by police. And FBI footwear expert William Bodziak said that defense witness Henry Lee had mistaken old tool marks for footprints at the scene and that only one set of shoe prints had led away from the scene—those made by a pair of size 12 Bruno Magli shoes. To counter the claim that Simpson was too crippled to commit the crimes, the prosecution showed a fitness video that Simpson had made shortly before the murders. Clark and Darden explained the missing socks in the video taken of Simpson's room by presenting proof that the police had shot the video after collecting the socks as evidence.

In their summary before the jury, the prosecutors recapped their case. Simpson had no alibi for the time of the murders. Allan Park did not find him at home until after the murders. Simpson had received a cut at about the time of the murders. Simpson's blood was found at the murder scene. Nicole and Goldman's blood was found on Simpson's property. And Simpson had a prior history of violent behavior toward his wife.

Prosecutors Clark and Darden argued that along with all the other supporting evidence, these six facts added up to overwhelming evidence of Simpson's guilt.

LEGAL ISSUES

Although the prosecution has charged O. J. Simpson with *first-degree murder*—murder deliberately planned and carried out—in the deaths of both Nicole Brown Simpson and Ronald Goldman, Judge Lance Ito instructed the jury that Simpson could be convicted of the lesser charge of second-degree murder if the facts warranted it. Rather than acquit him if jurors felt the prosecution had not proven that Simpson had committed first-degree murder, they could convict him of committing murders that he had not planned in advance.

Judge Ito acknowledged that the various witnesses had given very different interpretations of the evidence and descriptions of the events. To deal with the often conflicting testimony of the eyewitnesses and the expert witnesses, Judge Ito told the jurors that they alone must determine the witnesses' credibility. In deciding whom to believe, Ito advised them to consider the expertise, character, bias, and motive of witnesses.

YOU ARE THE JUROR.
WHAT IS YOUR DECISION?

After an exhausting eight months of being under the media spotlight and sequestered in a hotel, away from family and friends, the case is finally in your hands. What verdict do you declare in the murder charges against O. J. Simpson?

Option 1   **Simpson is not guilty.**

Option 2   **Simpson is guilty of two counts of first-degree murder.**

Option 3   **Simpson is guilty of two counts of second-degree murder.**

Option 4   **Simpson is guilty of one count of first-degree murder and one count of second-degree murder.**

The former football superstar and popular actor O. J. Simpson spent millions to defend himself against the double-murder charges. Johnnie Cochran, the leader of his defense "Dream Team," stands behind him.

The jurors chose *Option 1*. They found Simpson not guilty.

An initial vote among the jurors showed 10 in favor of a verdict of not guilty and only 2 in favor of a guilty verdict. Despite the fact that the trial had produced more than 45,000 pages of testimony, the jury deliberated for less than four hours before convincing the two holdouts that Simpson should go free.

The jurors, consisting of nine blacks, two whites, and one Hispanic, later insisted that their racial background had nothing to do with their decision. Juror Brenda Moran explained, "In plain English, the glove didn't fit."

Because of Judge Ito's insistence on weeding out jurors who knew anything about the case, the jury included few educated or well-read people. Only 2 of the 12 jurors had attended college. This lack of education may be one reason the jury ignored the complex and intricate DNA evidence that linked Simpson to the crime.

Although 10 of the 12 jurors were women, they also dismissed the evidence that Simpson had violently abused his wife as a waste of time. Instead, the jurors wanted to know why the police did not find more blood on Simpson's car and property, and they were suspicious of the testimony of detectives Fuhrman and Vannater. One juror, who later admitted that she thought Simpson was probably guilty, felt she had to give Simpson the benefit of the doubt after hearing Fuhrman's comments that all "niggers" should be burned. The jury also bought the defense's argument that the police had been sloppy in collecting and storing evidence. "Garbage in, garbage out," commented one juror.

ANALYSIS

Jury consultants noted that the jury had been strongly inclined to believe in Simpson's innocence before the trial began. On a pretrial questionnaire, three-fourths of the jurors replied that they thought Simpson was unlikely to commit murder because he had excelled at football.

A majority of Americans disagreed with the Simpson verdict. Perhaps no trial in history provoked more discussion of the fairness of the U.S. justice system. Wealthy people like Simpson can hire expensive lawyers and expert witnesses who can confuse uneducated jurors and win acquittals despite the evidence, while the poor are often convicted on much flimsier evidence.

The verdict also exposed an enormous gulf between black and white Americans. While the majority of white Americans believed that Simpson got away with murder, a large majority of African Americans believed him innocent and a victim of a police framing. The difference in black and white perceptions of the police has led to serious questions about whether police treat all citizens equally.

Although Simpson was acquitted of committing murder, in November 1996 the family of Ron Goldman took him to court in a civil trial for *wrongful death*. Nicole Simpson's family filed a survivorship suit, which put any compensation into a fund for Nicole's children. On February 4, 1997, the jury in this case decided that Simpson was responsible for the deaths of his ex-wife and Goldman. To make amends to Goldman's family and to punish Simpson for the murders, the jury awarded the Goldman family $8.5 million in compensatory damages (Nicole's family did not seek compensatory damages) and both families $25 million in punitive damages.

HOW A JURY IS CHOSEN

1. You are one of a large number of residents who received a summons to appear on a given date before the court for jury selection. (An unprecedented 1,000 people were called in Los Angeles County to be screened for the O. J. Simpson jury.)

2. Unless you have been excused from the jury because of the hardship jury duty would cause in your life— missed work, childcare, etc.—you and the other prospective jurors will respond to a questionnaire designed to reveal any biases you might have that would prevent you from giving the accused a fair trial.

3. If, based on your answers to the questionnaire, both the prosecution and the defense believe you could be an unbiased juror, you will be part of the jury panel from which the final 12 jurors and a varying number of alternates will be chosen.

4. Next, you and the other members of the jury panel will be called into the courtroom one by one for *voir dire*, or questioning by the lawyers to determine who they want to have on the jury. The lawyers will try to figure out whether you will be more inclined to favor the defense or the prosecution.

5. Once the voir dire questioning is over, any number of prospective jurors can be eliminated through *challenges for cause*, which include knowing someone involved in the trial or a range of other legal reasons that could prevent them from serving fairly on this

jury. The remaining jurors are called in one by one in random order. The prosecution and the defense attorneys each have a specified number of *peremptory challenges,* or chances to eliminate prospective jurors without giving a reason. They reject jurors based on their impression from voir dire about who might be unlikely to decide in their favor. Each juror who is not challenged at this point takes a seat on the jury until the 12 jurors and alternates have been selected. The alternates will sit in the jury box the length of the trial, but they will not be able to vote in jury deliberations unless they take the place of jurors who are unable to serve the length of the trial.

SOURCE NOTES

Quoted passages are noted by page and order of citation.

p. 13: Jim Fisher, *The Lindbergh Case* (New Brunswick, N.J.: Rutgers University Press, 1987).

p. 16: Sidney Whipple, *The Lindbergh Crime* (New York: Blue Ribbon, 1935).

pp. 20, 23, 26, 27 (both): Anita Gustafson, *Guilty or Innocent?* (New York: Holt, Rinehart, & Winston, 1985).

pp. 31, 32 (all), 33, 34 (all), 35, 40 (both), 41: Anthony Lewis, *Make No Law: The Sullivan Case and the First Amendment* (New York: Random House, 1991).

p. 36: Norman Dorsen, "Libel and the Free Press," *Nation*, January 27, 1964.

pp. 45, 58 (1st): Andrew David, *Famous Criminal Trials* (Minneapolis: Lerner, 1979).

pp. 47 (both), 48 (all), 50 (both), 51, 52 (both), 53, 54 (1st, 3rd), 58 (2nd), 60: John Schultz, *Motion Will Be Denied* (New York: Morrow, 1972).

p. 54 (2nd): Lee Arbetman, *Great Trials in American History* (St. Paul: West Publishing, 1985).

p. 62: "Which Patty to Believe?" *Time*, November 6, 1975.

pp. 64, 75: Janey Jimenez, *My Prisoner* (Kansas City: Sheed, Andrews & McMeel, 1977).

pp. 66 (1st), 68 (all), 69 (1st): "Battle over Patty's Mind," *Time*, March 8, 1976.

pp. 66 (2nd, 3rd), 69 (2nd), 70, 74 (1st, 2nd, 3rd): "The Verdict on Patty: Guilty as Charged," *Time*, March 29, 1976.

p. 74 (4th): F. Lee Bailey, "Why Patty's Trial Was Unfair," *Ladies Home Journal*, October 7, 1976.

pp. 79, 80 (1st), 84 (1st), 89, 91 (1st, 3rd): Randy Shilts, *The Mayor of Castro Street: The Life and Times of Harvey Milk* (New York: St. Martin's Press, 1982).

pp. 80 (2nd), 81, 82, 83 (2nd, 3rd), 84 (2nd), 91 (2nd): Michael Weiss, *Double Play* (Reading, Mass.: Addison-Wesley, 1984).

p. 83 (1st): "Getting Off," *Time*, May 28, 1979.

pp. 94, 98, 99, 102, 107: Lee Patrick Strobel, *Reckless Homicide* (South Bend, Ind.: And Books, 1980).

pp. 96, 101: "A Dead Stop in the Ford Pinto Trial?" *Newsweek*, February 25, 1980.

pp. 111, 115 (2nd, 3rd), 116, 118, 118-119, 122, 123: George P. Fletcher, *A Crime of Self-Defense* (New York: Free Press, 1988).

pp. 112, 113 (all), 114 (all), 115 (1st), 117: Mark Lesly, with Charles Shuttlesworth, *Subway Gunman: A Juror's Account of the Bernhard Goetz Trial* (New York: British American Publishing, 1988).

p. 127 (1st): televised court proceedings, January 31, 1995.

p. 127 (2nd): "He's Going Nuts," *Newsweek*, July 4, 1994.

p. 127 (3rd, 4th): televised court proceedings, February 7, 1995.

pp. 133, 134, 135, 140, 141: "Judgment Day," *Newsweek*, October 9, 1995.

p. 138: Associated Press, July 18, 1995.

p. 139: Gerald Uelmen, *Lessons from the Trial: The People v. O. J. Simpson* (Kansas City: Andrews & McMeel, 1996).

p. 145 (1st): "Perspectives," *Newsweek*, October 16, 1995.

p. 145 (2nd): Associated Press, October 5, 1995.

BIBLIOGRAPHY

Arbetman, Lee. *Great Trials in American History.* St. Paul: West Publishing, 1985.

Bailey, F. Lee. "Why Patty's Trial Was Unfair." *Ladies Home Journal*, October 7, 1976.

"Battle over Patty's Mind." *Time*, March 8, 1976.

Behn, Noel. *Lindbergh: The Crime.* New York: Atlantic Monthly Press, 1994.

Biema, David van. "The Burden of Evidence." *Time*, July 18, 1994.

David, Andrew. *Famous Criminal Trials.* Minneapolis: Lerner, 1979.

"A Dead Stop in the Ford Pinto Trial?" *Newsweek*, February 25, 1980.

Dorsen, Norman. "Libel and the Free Press." *Nation*, January 27, 1964.

"End Game." *Newsweek*, March 22, 1976.

Epstein, Jason. *The Great Conspiracy Trial.* New York: Random House, 1970.

Fisher, Jim. *The Lindbergh Case.* New Brunswick, N.J.: Rutgers University Press, 1987.

Fletcher, George P. *A Crime of Self-Defense.* New York: Free Press, 1988.

"Ford's Pinto: Not Guilty." *Newsweek*, March 24, 1980.

"Getting Off." *Time*, May 28, 1979.

Gustafson, Anita. *Guilty or Innocent?* New York: Holt, Rhinehart, & Winston, 1985.

Hearst, Patricia Campbell, with Alvin Moscow. *Every Secret Thing*. Garden City, N.Y.: Doubleday, 1982.

"He's Going Nuts." *Newsweek*, July 4, 1994.

"How the Jury Saw It." *Newsweek*, October 16, 1995.

Jimenez, Janey. *My Prisoner*. Kansas City: Sheed, Andrews & McMeel, 1977.

"Judgment Day." *Newsweek*, October 9, 1995.

Lesly, Mark, with Charles Shuttlesworth. *Subway Gunman: A Juror's Account of the Bernhard Goetz Trial*. New York: British American Publishing, 1988.

Lewis, Anthony. *Make No Law: The Sullivan Case and the First Amendment*. New York: Random House, 1991.

"Libel." *Time*, October 2, 1964.

Messick, Hank, and Burt Goldblatt. *Kidnapping: The Illustrated History*. New York: Dial, 1974.

"Now, a Jury of His Peers." *Time*, November 14, 1994.

"Perspectives." *Newsweek*, October 16, 1995.

Reibstein, Larry. "And Now, the Trial." *Newsweek*, January 25, 1995.

———. "Playing the Race Card." *Newsweek*, February 20, 1995.

"Run up to the Trial." *U.S. News & World Report*, July 18, 1994.

Schultz, John. *Motion Will Be Denied*. New York: Morrow, 1972.

Shilts, Randy. *The Mayor of Castro Street: The Life and Times of Harvey Milk*. New York: St. Martin's Press, 1982.

Strobel, Lee Patrick. *Reckless Homicide*. South Bend, Ind.: And Books, 1980.

"Strong Suspicion." *Newsweek*, July 19, 1994.

Sullivan, Randall. "Unreasonable Doubt." *Rolling Stone*, December 29, 1994.

"Three Faces of Patty." *Newsweek*, March 8, 1976.

Uelmen, Gerald. *Lessons from the Trial: The People v. O. J. Simpson*. Kansas City: Andrews & McMeel, 1996.

"The Verdict on Patty: Guilty as Charged." *Time*, March 29, 1976.

Weiss, Michael. *Double Play*. Reading, Mass.: Addison-Wesley, 1984.

———. "Trial and Error." *Rolling Stone*, July 12, 1979.

"Which Patty to Believe." *Time*, October 6, 1975.

Whipple, Sidney. *The Lindbergh Crime*. New York: Blue Ribbon, 1935.

INDEX

Slotnick, Barry, 115, 116, 117
Smith, Peter, 115
Sneva, Tom, 101
Solmon, George, 83
Staffeldt, Harold, 105, 107, 108-109
Stahl, David, 47
Stein, Robert, 96
Steiner, Robert E., 34
Stephens, Boyd, 79-80
Stubblebine, James, 69
Students for a Democratic Society, 46
"Subway Vigilante," 111. See also Goetz, Bernhard
Sullivan, L. B., 32, 33, 34, 35, 36, 37, 39; civil suit of, against New York Times, 30, 31, 40
Supreme Court: Alabama, 40-41; U.S., 12, 40-42
Symbionese Liberation Army (SLA), 61, 63, 64, 65, 66, 75; kidnapping of Patty Hearst by, 61, 62, 66, 69; treatment of Hearst by, 66-67, 68, 70

Tania (Hearst's alias), 65
Toms, Douglas, 101, 104
Trenchard, Thomas, 23, 25
"Twinkie defense," 82-83, 92

Ulrich, Donna, 93, 94; death of, in Pinto explosion, 93, 94
Ulrich, Earl, 99
Ulrich, Judy, 93, 94, 96, 97, 99-100; death of, in Pinto explosion, 93, 94, 99
Ulrich, Lyn, 93, 94, 96; death of, in Pinto explosion, 93, 94
Ulrich, Mattie, 98, 99
Ulrich, Sharon, 99

Vannater, Phil, 130-131, 135, 137-138, 145; testimony of, in Simpson case, 130-131
Vietnam War, 43-44, 67;

protest against, 44-45, 48, 49. See also Democratic National Convention, riots during
voir dire, 147, 148

Waples, Gregory, 112, 114, 118
Watergate hearings, 100
Weiner, Lee, 46, 56, 57
Weinglass, Leonard, 49, 50, 52-53
Wendel, Paul, 27
West, Louis, 68, 70
White, Dan, 88; affected by junk food, 82-84, 92; character of, 81-82, 86, 89, 91-92; confession of, 78, 79, 81; murder of Moscone and Milk by, 78, 79-80, 81, 83, 84, 85, 86, 92; suicide of, 92. See also White trial
White trial: background of, 77-78; controversy over verdict in, 90-91; decision of jury in, 89, 90; defense case in, 81-84; legal issues in, 86, 87; prosecution case in, 79-80, 91, 92; psychiatric testimony in, 82-84, 85; rebuttal in, 85; "Twinkie defense" in, 82-83, 92. See also White, Dan
Wilentz, David T., 8, 15, 17, 18
Wolfe, Willie, 70, 73
Woodard, Levi, Jr., 99
wrongful death, 146

Youth International Party, 46
Yudwitz, Bernard, 117
Yurgilas, James, 107, 108

Zenger, John Peter, trial of, 6
Zimring, Franklin E., 74

ABOUT THE AUTHOR

NATHAN AASENG is an award-winning author of over 100 fiction and nonfiction books for young readers. He writes on subjects ranging from science to business, government to law. Aaseng's books for The Oliver Press include *Treacherous Traitors*, *Great Justices of the Supreme Court*, *America's Third-Party Presidential Candidates*, *Genetics: Unlocking the Secrets of Life*, *You Are the President*, *You Are the President II*, *You Are the General*, *You Are the General II*, *You Are the Supreme Court Justice*, *You Are the Senator*, and *You Are the Corporate Executive*.